Investing Strategies:

Profitable and Updated

Tony POW

Why you want to read this book

It should improve your financial health substantially. There are about a million investment books. Why we need another one?

- I select proven ideas from more than 100 books besides my original ideas and experiences. I also include links to current articles that will bring more depth to the topic. It is not a novel or documenting the story of my life. All related chapters are grouped in a section for easy future reference. Some chapters are not easy to digest as they have a lot of pointers and some may require you to try them out yourself.

- A best seller was written by a young writer whose main income was from his books and none from his investing. His book is good for beginners or you want to brush up your English. Most of my incomes are from investing.

- Many popular books claiming the authors making millions. However, usually their techniques are hard to follow. Many admitted they had been bankrupted many times. Hence, their chance of bankrupting again is very high. Is bankruptcy fine with you? I cannot afford bankruptcy past and present. My techniques minimize risking my money.

- There are many popular books. They worked very well at one time and folks making millions following the advice. However, look at their recent performances of the last five years. Most of them cannot even beat the S&P 500 index.

- Check the recent mediocre performance of gurus such as Buffett. They are the market and they cannot beat themselves. Their techniques may no longer work.

- Check out my success stories.
  http://tonyp4idea.blogspot.com/2015/09/successes.html

Contents

Why you trust me

This book represents my years of investing experience, the hundreds of investing books I read and thousands of simulations. Hopefully this book will improve your financial health substantially as it has one to mine. I also hope that by reading this book you can become a better investor no matter if you are a **beginner or a fund manager**.

My children have no interest in investing, so I do not hold back anything. I expect my readers will do better financially if they can avoid my mistakes that I will point out in this book. Today and at my age I am a very conservative investor and am doing well with my investments. I wish I could have tried out many of my strategies earlier in my investing life.

- My simple technique that does not use chart told us to **exit the market** on March, 14, 2022.

- I had a 50% return in one month in 2018 by using my year-end strategy. I would challenge any investor with this type of monthly return in a diversified portfolio of 8 stocks or more.

- I recommended 20 stocks in an article titled Amazing Return in Seeking Alpha. If you bought them on the published date, you would have beaten the S&P 500 index by more than 100% in a year without considering dividends as demonstrated in my other article A Tale of Two Portfolios.

  I challenge anyone who has a better one-year performance by recommending a diversified portfolio of 15 or more stocks in any publication.

- In 01/2016, I recommended buying OIL in my posts in Seeking Alpha's Wall Street Breakfast and my blog when oil was less than $30 per barrel.
  http://tonyp4idea.blogspot.com/2016/01/oil-price.html.

- Recommended Apple at $55.72 (1-7 split adjusted) on April 19, 2013 as the only example in my book Scoring Stocks and I recommended selling it at $132 in 2/2015 with valid arguments described in this link.
  http://tonyp4idea.blogspot.com/2015/02/dump-apple.html

Why you invest

You will need to learn about investing sooner or later in your life. You also need to take some calculated risks.

Compare the returns of the following assets: cash, CDs, treasury bills, bonds, real estate and stocks. We start with the risk-free investments and end with the riskiest. It turns out that the average returns are in the opposite order. Cash and CDs are not risk-free as inflation eats our profits. For example, the real return is negative for the 2% return in a CD and a 3% inflation rate. In addition, you have to pay taxes for the 'returns'. Our capitalist system punishes us for not taking risks. However, protect your portfolio such as using stop orders and not using leverages including options for beginners. Start being a turtle investor rather than a trader that could lose all your money.

There are two kinds of risk: blind risk and calculated risk. If you buy a stock due to a recommendation from a commentator on TV or a tip, most likely you are taking a blind risk. It would be the same in buying a house without thoroughly evaluating the house and its neighborhood. When you buy stocks with a proven strategy (i.e., when/what stocks to buy and when/what stocks to sell), you are taking a calculated risk. In the long run, stocks with calculated and educated risks are profitable.

Be a turtle investor by investing in value stocks and holding for longer time periods (a year or more). "Buy and Monitor" is a better approach than "Buy and Hold" as some could lose all the stocks' value such as in the failure of Enron.

For experienced investors, shorting, short-term trading and covered calls would make you good profits. Simple market timing would reduce your losses during market downturns. If you buy a market ETF and use my simple market timing, you should have beaten the market by a wide margin from 2000 to 2019.

With so many fraudulent and poor managed hedge funds (but many exceptions), do not trust anyone with your investing. Do not buy investing instruments that are highly marketed such as annuity and term insurance.

If you are a handy man and do not mind to satisfy the constant requests of your tenants, buy real estate in growing areas that could be very profitable in the long run. Take advantage of the tax laws such as investing in a 401K especially the part that is matched by your company and/or a Roth IRA.

How to beat the S&P500 index by 100%

I recommended 20 stocks in an article Amazing Return in Seeking Alpha, a web site for investors. If you bought them on the published date and then you would have beaten the S&P500 index by over 100% without considering dividends as demonstrated in my other article A Tale of Two Portfolios. One of the many techniques is my Pow P/E as illustrated in another article The Mysteries of P/E.

Let's say I made a mistake and it is only a 10% gain. How many fund managers can beat the S&P500 index by 10% regularly?

Introduction

A strategy is how to find stocks (usually via screens, also known as searches), analyze the stocks, buy them and sell them. This section concentrates on screening for stocks.

I prefer value stocks (i.e., based on fundamentals). However, fundamentals are secondary for some strategies such as momentum. This book uses the same techniques in Finding Stocks and Scoring Stocks, so they will not be repeated here.

This book describes some simpler strategies and leaves the complicated ones in their own books that follow.

I read the book "What Works on Wall Street" by James O'Shaughnessy blaming many other strategies for non-performance. Later I read another book mentioning that O'Shaughnessy did not work after he published his book.

As mentioned previously, the strategy will not be effective when there are too many followers. That's the reason I provide you with many strategies and you should explore newer strategies yourself. The market favors different groups of strategies in different stages of the market cycle.

The best way to check what is the favorable strategy is to test the performances of your different strategies for the last three to six months. Several low-cost subscription services provide historical databases to make this task simple and feasible.

Traders and hedge fund managers change their strategies frequently. Retail investors should do the same.

One strategy was the poster boy for a subscription service. It worked well before. I tested it recently and it was one of the worst strategies. The lesson is: There are no evergreen strategies. Test out whether they still work in the last 90 days.

This book is divided into 2 books plus the Bonus. I started with the Simple Techniques and then the Basic Investing Strategies. More advanced strategies are described in separate books that are all included in this book.

A sample strategy

It is an example. Adjust it to your preferences and requirements. Instead of buying stocks, just save them in a watch list and buy them when the entire market is on sale. It consists of the following three steps.

1. When to search stocks to be traded. For example, it is once a month when the market is not risky.
2. What to buy. It will be described in more detail later.
3. Sell the stock(s). When the market is plunging, your objectives have been satisfied, or the bought stock(s) does not satisfy most criteria described in #2.

Step #2. There are several steps: Fundamental Analysis, Intangible Analysis, Qualitative Analysis and Technical Analysis.

For simplicity, stick with Fundamental Analysis here. The stocks have to satisfy most of the following criteria. Try to use a screener to limit your selection. If you do not find any stock, relax the criteria or do nothing as the market may be peaking and/or expensive. Skip those criteria that you do not have a subscription to access to.

- It must be in one of the three major U.S. exchanges. No ADRs and partnerships (unless you're an expert in the countries/fields).
- Market Cap is over 100 M (or over 10B for blue chips).
- Price is over $2.
- Average daily volume must be at least 20 times more than your potential position.
- Expected P/E is less than 20 and E must be positive.
- P/Cash Flow is less than 25 and Cash Flow must be positive.
- Debt/Equity is less than 1 (preferable .5; also depending on specific industry).
- Fidelity's Analyst Opinion is 7 or higher.
- Piotroski's (from GuruFocus or other sources) F-Score is 7 or higher.

Fidelity Video:
Trading strategies
https://www.fidelity.com/learning-center/trading/types-of-trading-strategies/overview

Dedication

To all retail investors and future retail investors including my grandchildren.

Acknowledgement

Thanks to Seeking Alpha, Wikipedia and Investopedia for the many helpful links to enrich this book. Yahoo! Finance and Finviz.com for the tools and charts used in this book.

Important notices © 2014-23 Tony POW. Emails to pow_tony@yahoo.com

Version	Paperback	Kindle
1.0	02/14	02/14
2.5	12/16	12/16
3.0	11/19	11/19
3.2	04/22	04/23

Disclaimer

Do not gamble with money that you cannot afford to lose. Past performance is a guideline and is not necessarily indicative of future results. All information is believed to be accurate, but there is not a guarantee. All the strategies including charts to detect market plunges described have no guarantee that they will make money and they may lose money. Do not trade without doing due diligence and be warned that most data may be obsolete. All my articles and the associated data are for informational and illustration purposes only. I'm not a professional investment counselor, a tax professional or any other field. Seek one before you make any investment decisions. Remember to consult with a registered financial adviser before making any investment decisions. The above mentioned also applies for all other advice such as on accounting, taxes, health and any topic mentioned in this book. Tax laws change all the time, so talk to your tax advisors before taking any action. Some articles may offend some one or some organization unintentionally. If I did, I'm sorry about that. I am politically and religiously neutral. I have provided my best efforts to ensure the accuracy of my articles. Data also from different sources was believed to be accurate. However, there is no guarantee that they are accurate and suitable for the current market conditions and /or your individual situations. The values of some parameters such as RSI(14) are arbitrarily set by me. I have made a lot of predictions that may not materialize. My publisher and I are not liable for any damages in using this book or its contents.

How the rate of return is calculated

They are for education purposes only, and do not make your investing decisions based on them. I usually use annualized for better comparisons; 4% in a month is more than 5% in a year for example. For short-term strategies including momentum, shorting and year-end strategy, I use the returns for a month, and sometimes including returns for 2 months for comparison. Annualized returns are usually used for long-term strategies. The holding periods may have a few days off due to holidays and weekends. For simplicity, most of my returns do not include commissions, exchange fees, order spread and dividends. Most numbers have been rounded up for better readability. The return = profit / investment. I and my publisher are not liable for any error. I use SPY and sometimes RSP as a yardstick; RSP and SPY have the same S&P 500 stocks, but the stocks are weighed evenly in RSP. However, many readers do not know RSP.

How to use this book

Do not trade the stocks discussed in this book, as they may be outdated. Learn the reasons they are recommended.

This book is not a novel that you should read sequentially. This book is organized as a reference book. You can start any chapter or find the related topic as needed. I recommend starting to glance at the table of contents if available.

Most graphs and tables are in landscape orientation (recommended for small screens) for both paperback and e-readers. Some graphs may not be displayed adequately on a small screen of an e-reader. Use a PC to read the graphs on the larger screen. For better orientation, just flip your e-reader device 90 degrees if it is available. Most e-readers let you select a table or a graph to display it to fit the screen.

The **font size** (Ctrl Minus for browser implementation of e-readers) should be adjustable for e-books.

There are clickable links to web articles and/or YouTube videos, which are usually more entertaining. Most of them are from public websites such as Wikipedia. Some public links may not be available in the future as they are not under my control and my book may change. For security, get the information such as "RSI(14)" directly from the source; the primary ones are Wikipedia, Investopedia, YouTube and Fidelity.

These links extend the usefulness of this book by making available specific topics that may not be interesting to every reader. It also provides articles (most are not written by me) for more in-depth analysis. Instead of typing the links to your browser, you can access the following website to access most of the links easier. One reader commented, "(the links have) lots of useful information. The author also has a sense of humor." http://tonyp4idea.blogspot.com/2021/05/web-links-for-printed-copy-of-my-book.html

Fidelity provides video clips to explain some of the basic terms. Fidelity does not require a balance to open an account; I have no affiliation with them except I retired from Fidelity. Take advantage of their extensive research and info. YouTube offers similar video lessons. This book provides many of the links for the paperback readers. In any case, get the same information or extra information by entering a search in Wikipedia and/or Investopedia (http://www.investopedia.com/) such as "Dogs of the Dow".

'Afterthoughts' includes my additional comments and ideas of minor importance. There are fillers with tips, refreshing pictures (most were taken by me) and jokes (most original) to fill up some empty space of the printed book. Fillers, links and afterthoughts should not disrupt the flow of reading this book. One user commented on my fillers: "Thanks for the jabs (Fillers) to make the reading fun while getting an education".

For convenience, this book uses SPY, an Exchange Traded Fund (ETF) simulating the S&P 500, as the benchmark for the market.

Since most of the stock recommendations are probably obsolete by the time you read about them, use them as examples and do not trade the mentioned stocks without consulting your financial advisor first. For simplicity, I treat ETN the same as ETF.

Summary

This book is lengthy with a lot of information on strategies. I have used some of them based on the current market conditions and my own requirements. I include some strategies that I believe they have values. For just a moment, forget everything you've learned here and elsewhere on strategies and use your common sense to see whether the following makes sense to you.

- Evaluate your requirements and select the strategy or strategies you want. Test them thoroughly on paper before committing real money.
- Need to check the recent performance of your screens. There are no evergreen strategies that I know of. This is why many gurus have failed in 2015 (and so far in the first part of 2016) as the market changed.
- Some strategies perform better in up markets and vice versa.
- Stick with my three-step process: Market Timing, Screen Stocks and Evaluate Stocks.
  When the market is risky, do not buy stocks. "Strategy" is the first part of Screening Stocks and the second part is when and why to sell stocks. You need to provide exit strategies such as stop orders to reduce further losses.
- Some strategies perform better for holding stocks short term (3 months or less), while some (most based on value) perform better in the longer term (12 months or more).
- Some strategies perform better in a specific stage of a market cycle. Select several strategies for paper trading. Use the one that performs best in the last month or two. It could continue the performance in the coming month. In any case, use stops to protect your investments.

Filler: CIA mistook it as a missile silo in China.

Book 1: Simple Techniques

For starters, just trade ETFs such as SPY (an ETF simulating the market), and you can skip the rest of the book. It only takes a few minutes every month. When the market is not plunging, buy or keep SPY (or any ETF that stimulates the market); otherwise sell it. Do the opposite when the market is recovering.

If you have less than $50,000 to invest, just buy ETFs. Improve your investing skills by reading investment articles from this book and your broker's website. For example, Fidelity has a lot of information for investors.

Subscription to AAII is recommended. When your portfolio grows more than $50,000, invest on a subscription such as Value Line, GuruFocus, Zacks or IBD (more for momentum traders). Initially, use the information for paper trading on value stocks, which is usually available from brokers.

For the long term, knowledge is most important in your investing life and experience comes next. Retail investors have a lot of advantages over fund managers. However, I advise you NOT to be a trader. Hence, you should ignore the 'fabulous' trade systems that claim to be very profitable. Statistically most amateur traders lose money as they cannot compete with experienced, disciplined traders.

How to start

I recommend trading ETFs first and when the market is not risky. The very basic terms such as ETF are not fully explained here; try Investopedia for terms you need to know. Otherwise, this book would be doubled in size and it would bore most readers. Investopedia, your broker's website (especially Fidelity) and AAII (requiring subscription) provide many excellent articles. Alternatively, buy a book for beginners. Here are some freebies:

Click here for Morningstar classroom.
http://morningstar.com/cover/classroom.html
Click here for Vanguard.
https://investor.vanguard.com/investing/investor-education
Click here for Investopedia's Tutorials.
http://www.investopedia.com/university/
Click here for Yahoo!
http://finance.yahoo.com/education/begin_investing
Click here for Fidelity basic in investing.
https://www.fidelity.com/investment-guidance/investing-basics

1   Simplest market timing

Why market timing
Before 2000, market timing was a waste of time. However, after that, we have had two market plunges with the average loss of about 45%. It sounds harder to time the market than it actually is. We have a simple technique to detect market plunges and when to reenter the market. Our objective is reducing the loss to 25%.

Market timing depends on charts; the following describes how to use chart information without creating charts. Most charts will not identify the peaks and bottoms of the market as they depend on data (i.e., the stock prices). However, it would reduce further losses. It is simpler than it sounds. Just follow the procedure below.

The first part of this technique detects potential market plunges, and the second part advises you when to start reentering the market. It applies to individual stocks too. It also works to detect the trend of a sector (entering an ETF for the specific sector instead of SPY) and a specific stock.

Step-by-step procedure
When the market timer indicator (Death Cross) described next tells you to exit the market, sell SPY (an ETF simulating S&P 500). Do not forget to buy back SPY or similar ETF such as RSP, when the indicator (Golden Cross) tells you to return.

My experiences in 2000s
Basically I did the same as the above with some adaptations. I worked for a mutual fund company and they did not allow me to trade stocks effectively. However, I was allowed to trade sector funds offered by the company. Every two months, I switched to the sectors with the best performances for the last month. When most sectors were down for the last month, I rotated them to the money market fund. In March or April, 2000, I switched to traditional sectors from high-tech sectors (better to switch to market money fund). During the time, I bought those stocks that had cash enough to last more than two years judging by their burn rates. The indicators should do a better job.

How to detect market plunges without charts (similar to Death Cross)
1.   Bring up Finviz.com.

2. Enter SPY (or any ETF that simulates the market) or RSP for equally weighed SPY.
3. If SMA-200% is positive, it indicates that the market plunge has not been detected and you can skip the following steps.
4. The market is plunging if SMA-50% is more negative than SMA-200%. To illustrate this condition, SMA-200% is -2% and SMA-50% is -5%.
5. Conservative investors should sell most stocks starting with the riskiest ones first such as the ones with negative earnings, high P/Es and/or high Debt/Equity. Obtain this info from Finviz.com by entering the symbol of the stock you own.
6. Aggressive investors should sell all stocks. Extremely aggressive investors should sell all stocks, buy contra ETFs, and even short stocks. I do not recommend beginners to be aggressive.

Example

As of 2/12/2022, the following are from Finviz.com.

ETF	SMA-200	SMA-50	SMA-20	Death Cross?
SPY	-0.8%	-4.2%	-1.7%	Yes (Step #4)
RSP	-0.5%	-1.9%	0.4%	Yes (Step #4)

Both ETFs indicate the market is a confirmed crash from my indications using a technique similar to Death Cross. However, they are quite close, and we should keep an eye on these numbers. In this case, SMA-20 has not been used. If it is a false alarm, the Golden Cross would indicate it and you should return to equity; it could be quite common in volatile markets. The futures indicate that on Monday (2/14/22) the market would plunge further.

Another test is using SMA-350: When the current price is below SMA-300, it is a crash. SMA-20 has to be more negative than SMA-50 and it has not been used here.

When to return to the market (similar to Golden Cross)

Use the above in a reversed sense to detect whether the market has been recovering. However, when the SMA-200% turns positive, I would start buying value stocks (low P/E but the 'E' has to be positive, and/or low Debt/Equity).

1. Bring up Finviz.com.
2. Enter SPY (or any ETF that simulates the market).
3. If SMA-200% is negative, the market is not recovering, and you can skip the following steps.
4. Sell all contra ETFs and close all shorts if you have any.

5. Market recovery is confirmed when SMA-50% is more positive than SMA-200%. To illustrate this condition, SMA-200% is 2% and SMA-50% is 5%. Commit a large percent of cash (or all cash for aggressive investors) to stocks. If you do not know what to buy, buy SPY or an ETF that simulates the market.

How often should you check the market timing indicators?

Do the above once a month. When the SPY price is closer to SMA actions percentage, perform the above once a week. The charts and data for market timing described in this book are based on SMA-350 (Simple Moving Average) that is more preferable than this simple procedure, but it requires some simple charting.

Nothing is perfect

If the market timing is perfect, there would be no poor folks. The major 'defects' are:

- It does not detect the peak / bottom as it depends on past data. However, it would save you a lot during the crash.
- It is hard to determine whether it is a correction or a crash.
- From 2000 to 2010, there was only one false signal. The indicator tells you to exit and then tells you to reenter the market shortly. In most cases, you do not lose a lot. After 2010, we have more false signals.
- The market may not be rational or may be influenced due to specific conditions such as excessive printing of USD. If you do not mind charting, use SMA 350 (or 400) using SPY. Buy when the price is above SMA-350 (or SMA-400), and sell otherwise. SMA-400 reduces the number of false signals, but it is not nimble.

#Filler: Glad to be an investor

After watching the following YouTube video, I am glad my parents did not push me to play piano and also glad I do not have any musical gene. How can I compete with this kid?

https://www.youtube.com/watch?v=yf0B4rVoq44

Also, glad not into some life-threatening professions such as surgical doctors, soldiers, fire fighters, etc. I can make mistakes in investing from time to time without suffering from the consequences. With the uptrend market for most of the last 50 years, most investors should make good money. Thank God.

2   Quick analysis of ETFs

Evaluate an ETF

ETFs are a basket of stocks according to the market, a specific sector, country or a specific theme.

Yahoo!Finance used to give the P/E of an ETF. Try to get it from ETFdb.com. Enter the symbol of the ETF such as XLU, and then select Valuation. If it is below 15 and above zero, it could be a value ETF. Also, if the current price is lower than its NAV, it is sold at a discount (or premium vice versa). Compare its YTD Return to SPY's.

Alternatively, get similar info from http://www.multpl.com/. In addition, this website provides the following metrics: Shiller P/E, Price/Sales, and Price/Book.

From Finviz.com, enter the ETF symbol. If SMA-20%, SMA-50% and SMA-200% are all positive, most likely the ETF is in an uptrend. To illustrate, SMA-200 is Simple Moving Average for the last 200 trading sessions (no trading on weekends and specific holidays). The percent is how much the stock price of the ETF is above the SMA. If the percent is negative, it means the stock price is below the SMA.

If your average holding period of your stocks is about 50 days, SMA-50% is more appropriate to you.

If RSI(14) > 65, it is probably oversold; if it is < 30, it is probably under-sold (indicating value).

In addition, ensure the ETF's average volume is high (I suggest more than 10,000 shares), the market cap is more than 300 M, and it has low fees. Most popular ETFs have these characteristics. Beginners should avoid leveraged ETFs.

How to determine if the sector has been recovered

It is easier to profit by following the uptrend of an ETF using the above info. It is hard to detect when the bottom of an ETF has been reached. If SMA-20%, SMA-50% and SMA-200% are all positive, most likely the ETF is in an uptrend or it has recovered. It does not always happen as predicted, so use stops to protect your investment.

An example

First, determine whether the market is risky. Most beginners should not invest in a risky market. Advanced investors can bet against the market or a specific sector by buying contra ETFs or puts.

Next, you want to limit the number of sector ETFs by selecting those that are either in an uptrend or hitting bottom (bottom is hard to predict). Personally, I prefer sectors with long-term uptrends (indicated by articles found in many websites including cnnfn.com and Seeking Alpha.

For illustration purposes only for deteriorating market conditions, I would select the following ETFs: SPY (simulating the market based on large companies) and XLP (consumer staples). XLP should perform better than XLY (consumer discretionary) during a recession as those products are the necessities.

Technical indicators such as SMA-50 (Simple Moving Average for the last 50 sessions), SMA-200 and RSI(14) are obtained from Finviz.com and the rest are obtained from Yahoo!Finance.com. After you buy the ETF, use a stop loss to protect your investment. For example, biotech sector moved up for many months until it crashed in 2015. Change the stop loss value every month to protect your gains in this case.

As of 2/5/2016	SPY	XLP (staples)	XLY (discreet.)
Price	190	50	71
NAV	192	50	73
• Technical			
SMA-50	-4%	0%	-7%
SMA-200	-6%	2%	-7%
RSI(14)	44	50	36
Other	Double bottom at $186		
• Fundamental			
P/E	17	20	19
Yield	2.1%	2.5%	1.5%
YTD return	-5%	0.5%	-5%
Net asset	174 B	9 B	10 B

Explanation

- The figures may not be identical among websites due to the dates they are using.
- XLY has the best discount among the 3 ETFs as most investors believe a recession is coming.
- XLP has less down trend among the 3 ETFs as expected.
- XLY is more undersold among the three as expected.
- Double bottom is a technical pattern that indicates the stock would surge upward.
- SPY has a better value according to its P/E.
- XLY's dividend is the least among the three as they have more tech companies in the ETF. They have to plow back the profits to research and development.
- XLP has the best YTD return among the three.
- As long as the asset is above 500 M (200 M for specialized ETFs), it is fine and all three pass this mark.

There are many metrics such as Debt/Equity not readily available from most websites. Many sites list the top holdings of a specific ETF. Just average the metrics of the top ten or so of its stock holdings.

#Filler: Illogical logic

If we do not test for the pandemic, we would have zero increase in this pandemic. Some silly folks buy this argument. What happens to the once-great country?

Filler: The problems of the U.S.

1. Our political system. We waste time arguing between the two parties. There is no long-term planning, as the other party could claim the credit. Same as corporations' CEOs who care about their yearly bonuses.
2. The politicians have to satisfy their voters. Today give them free cash by jacking up the printing press. And ignore the long-term consequences.
3. We have to protect our workers, our environment... Hence, we cannot compete with many countries.
4. We have spent too much on the military and ignore our crumbling infrastructure.
5. Historically no country can rule the world forever.
6. We blame China, but ignore how hard-working Chinese are.

An example

This example evaluates RING, a gold miner, using ETFdb and Finviz that are free from the web. The data is from July, 6, 2020.

Bring up ETFdb and enter RING in the search. There is basic info that are important to me: Sector (gold miners), Asset Size (Large-Cap), Issuer (iShares), Inception (Jan. 31, 2012), Expense Ratio (0.39%) and Tax Form (1099).

They fit all my requirements. The expense ratio is higher than most ETFs that simulate an index such as SPY. I try to trade ETFs using Tax Form 1099 in my taxable accounts. The large cap created about 8 years ago by a reputable company is good.

Select "Dividend and Valuation". P/E of 17.39 is fine in a rank of 11 in 27 in a similar group of ETFs. As in my books, I stated it is hard to evaluate miners. I buy this ETF primarily to fight the possibility of inflation and the potential depreciation of USD. The dividend rate of 0.52% (0.70% from Finviz) is in the low range of the scale; it is fine for me as dividend is not my concern.

There is more info from this website. For simplicity, bring up Finviz:
- The short-term trend is up (SMA-20% = 8% and SMA-50% = 7%).
- The long-term trend is up (SMA-200% = 26%).
- It is close to overbought (RSI(14) = 64%; 65% to me is overbought).
- It is -4% from 52-w High. It has performed well from the YTD, Last Year, Last Quarter, Last Month and Last Week.
- It almost doubled in price from mid-March this year.
- Avg. Vol. is fine.

From ETFdb, check the Holding. It has 39 stocks, so it is quite diversified for this industry. The two top holdings are NEM (19%) and ABX (18%), which is listed as GOLD in NYSX. I also consider buying these two stocks in addition to RING. You can estimate the other metrics that are not available by averaging these two stocks. Here is my summary:

STOCK	NEM	GOLD
Forward P/E	20	25
Debt / Share	0.31	0.24
ROE	17%	22%
Sales Q/Q	43%	30%
EPS Q/Q	389%	254%
SMA50	2%	4%
RSI(14)	59%	60%
Insider Trans	-13%	N/A

Fidelity's Equity Summary Score	6.1	6.8

3   Rotate four ETFs

We can beat the market by rotating one ETF that represents the market such as SPY and cash via market timing. Aggressive investors can add SH or PSQ (contra ETFs) to the four to have better returns during market plunges.

During a market uptrend, rotating the following four ETFs could be more profitable than staying with SPY (or any ETF that simulates the market). Be warned that a short-term capital gain in taxable accounts is not treated as favorably as the long-term capital gain; check current tax laws.

The allocation percentages depend on your individual risk tolerance. You can use indexed mutual funds. Compare their expenses and restrictions. Some mutual funds charge you if you withdraw within a specific time period.

Select the best performer of last month (from Seeking Alpha, cnnFn, or one of many ETF/mutual fund sites). Add a contra ETF such as SH to take advantage of a falling market for more aggressive investors. Add sector ETFs to the described four ETFs such as XLY, XLP, XLE, XLF, XLU, IYW, XHB, IYM, OIL and XLU to expand your selection.

ETFs	Money Market	U.S.	International	Bond
Fidelity		Spartan Total Market	Spartan Global Market	Spartan US Bond
Vanguard		Total Stock Market	Total International Market	Total Bond Market
My choice	Fidelity	SPY	Vanguard	Fidelity
Suggest %				
During Market plunge	90%	0%	0%	10%
After plunge	10%	60%	20%	10%

Explanation

- The above are suggestions only. If your broker offers similar ETFs, consider using them.
- Check out any restrictions of the ETFs and commissions.
- 4 ETFs (one actually is a money market fund) are enough for most starters. They are diversified, low-cost and you do not need rebalancing except during a market plunge.
- The percentages are suggestions only. If you are less risk tolerant, allocate more to a money market fund, CD and/or bond ETF.
- Have at least 10% allocated to the money market fund for safety.
- When the market is risky, reduce stock equities (i.e., increase money market and bond allocations).
- The symbols for Fidelity ETFs are FSTMX, FSGDX and FBIDX.
- The symbols for Vanguard ETFs are VTSMX, VGTSX and VBMFX.
- If you are more advanced, use additional sector ETFs to rotate. Also buy long-term bond funds (such as 30-year Treasury) when the interest rate is 10% or more.

#Filler: Where common sense is not common sense

Excessive printing of money is not a long-term solution. Servicing the huge debt weakens our competitiveness. The politicians just want to buy votes today and finance their campaigns. Our next generations have to pay for these huge debts.

#Filler: Cayman Island

Most global corporations are making fun of our tax system. Moving the "headquarter" to low-tax countries such as Cayman Island with a mailbox, a bank account and/or an office that has never been used is a norm. The profitable Boeing has negative tax liability. What a shame!

4   Simplest ways to evaluate stocks

Beginners should trade ETFs only. This chapter is for the readers who are ready or getting ready to trade stocks. In general, ETFs are diversified, less volatile than trading stocks. However, stocks offer higher profit but higher risk.

Many stock researches have already been done recently and some are available free of charge. I have no affiliation with Fidelity except I retired from it. You can open an account with them with no balance. Their Equity Summary Score is one of the best indicators; I check out **value** stocks with scores higher than 8. Concentrate on fundamental metrics such as P/E for long-term holds, and momentum metrics for short-term holds. Add criteria to limit the number of screened stocks. Finviz.com is a free screener.

Several sources

The popular ones are Morningstar, Value Line, The Street and Zacks (currently free for rankings of individual stocks). If they are not free, check out whether they are available from your local library. I have 3 simple ways to evaluate stocks starting with the simplest. In addition, read the articles on the selected stocks from Fidelity, Finviz, Seeking Alpha and many other sources for further evaluation.

Fidelity

Select only stocks that have Fidelity's Equity Summary Score 8 or higher. There is tons of information about a stock. Once in a while I did not agree with this score such as SHOP and ZM that scored high in August, 2020. Include the following for your analysis.

A modified stock selection based on a magazine article

Most metrics are available from Finviz except EV/EBITDA.

1. Forward P/E (expected earnings and not based on the last twelve months). It should range from 5 to 15 (10 to 25 for high tech stocks). EV/EBITDA (from Yahoo!Finance) is a better choice as it includes the debts and cash than P/E; it would be more effective if it uses forward earnings. If you do not use

EV/EBITDA, ensure Debt/Equity is less than 0.5 except for the debt-intensive industries.

2. ROE (Return of Equity) measures how well the company uses the capital. I prefer stocks with ROE greater than 5%.

3. Volatility. Conservative investors should select stocks with a beta of less than one (i.e., less volatile).

4. Insider Transactions for sales (i.e., negative) should be less than 5%. If it is -5%, most likely the insiders are dumping it.

5. Compare the metrics such as P/E and Debt/Equity to its five-year average and its competitors (available in Fidelity).

6. Momentum. Check out the SMA-50 (actually SMA-50%) and SMA-200. Ideally, they should be positive. SMA-50% is especially important for stocks you do not want to keep for a long time.

7. Check out articles on the stock as some recent events (for example a new lawsuit) have not been included in the metrics.

8. Compare the trend of the sector this stock is in. Under Finviz, enter the related sector ETF.

Summary
The sources are Fidelity (Equity Summary Score and various comparisons), Finviz and Yahoo!Finance (for EV/EBITDA). Value stocks should be held longer.

Category	Score / Metric	Value /Momentum
Score	Fidelity's Equity Summary Score	Both
Value	EV/EBITDA	Value
	P/E cheaper compared to 5-year avg.	Value
	P/E cheaper compared to its sector.	Value
	Insider Purchases	Both
Safety	Debt/Equity	Value

	Compare it to its sector.	Value
Momentum	50-SMA%	Momentum
	200-SMA% (for long term holds).	Value
Articles	Check out latest events	Both
Market	No purchase if market is risky.	Momentum

A simple scoring system using Finviz

Bring up Finviz.com and then enter the stock symbol.

No.	Metric	Good	Bad	Score
1	Forward P/E[1]	Between 2.5 and 12.5, Score = 2	> 50 or < 0, Score = -1	
2	P/ FCF[1]	< 12, Score = 1	>30 or < 0, Score = -1	
3	P/S[1]	< 0.8, Score = 1	< 0, Score = -1	
4	P/ B[1]	< 1, Score = 1	< 0, Score = -1	
	Compare quarter to quarter of last year			
5	Sales Q/Q	> 15%, Score = 1	< 0, Score = -1	
6	EPS Q/Q	> 20% , Score = 1	< 0, Score = -1	
			Grand Score	
	Stock Symbol Date[2]	Current Price	SPY	

Footnote

[1] Negative values for Sales (due to accounting adjustments), Equity and Book are possible but not likely.

[2] The last row is for your information only. SPY is used to measure whether it will beat the market by comparing the return of this stock to the return of SPY.

The Score

Score each metric and sum up all the scores giving the Grand Score. If the Grand Score is 3, the stock passes this scoring system. Even if it is a 2, it still deserves further analysis if you have time. You may want to add scores from other vendors. To illustrate on using Fidelity, add 1 to the score if Fidelity's Equity Summary score is 8 or higher. Monitor the performance after every 6 months or so to see whether this scoring system beats the market.

Very basic advice for beginners

Beginners should stick with U.S. stocks with Market Cap greater than 800 M (million), Debt/Equity less than .25 (25%) except for debt-intensive industries such as utilities and airlines and Forward P/E between 5 to 20 (25 for high-tech companies). These metrics are all available from Finviz.com, which is free.

Do not have more than 20% of your portfolio in one stock (unless it is an ETF or mutual fund) and do not have more than 30% of your portfolio in one sector.

For more conservative investors, buy non-volatile stocks whose beta (available from Yahoo!Finance) is less than 1. Beta of 1 represents the market (the S&P 500 index). For example, a stock with beta 1.5 statistically fluctuates more than 50% of the market and hence it is very volatile.

Try paper trading to check out your strategy and your skill in trading stocks. If your broker does not provide one, use a spreadsheet to record your trades or check the availability of simulator.investopedia.com.

#Filler: Silence is golden

I am glad I did not give advice to a friend who had to decide whether to take a lump sum payment or an annuity. The correction in March, 2020 would wipe out a lot of his portfolio if he took the lump sum payment. No one would share his profits when the predictions are correct, but the blame if it does not materialize.

It is the same in investing that nothing is certain. With educated guesses, we should have more rights than wrongs especially in the long run.

5   Simplest technical analysis

When the stock, the sector that the stock is in and the market are all above its SMA-N averages (Single Moving Average for the last N sessions), most likely the stock is trending up.

1. Bring up Finviz.com from your browser.

2. Enter SPY. Write down the SMA-200 (Single Moving Average for 200 sessions). Positive numbers indicate that the trend for the market is up.

    However, the market could be peaking or overbought. Be careful when SMA-200 is over 5% and / or RSI(14) is over 65%. RSI is a metric on overbought / underbought.

3. Enter the sector ETF the stock is in. Write down the SMA-50. Positive numbers indicate that trend for the sector is up.

    However, the sector could be peaking or overbought. Be careful when the SMA-200 is over 10% and / or RSI(14) is over 65%.

4. Enter the stock symbol. If your average holding period of the stocks is 200, use SMA-200 and so on. I recommend SMA-200 for holding value stocks long term and SMA-50 for momentum stocks. Write down the SMA-N for your stock. Positive numbers indicate that the trend is up.

    However, the stock could be peaking or overbought. Be careful when the SMA-200 (or SMA-50) is over 25% and / or RSI(14) is over 65%.

If the above three criteria and the fundamental criteria are satisfied, most likely it is a good buy. If you buy sector ETFs or mutual funds only, you can skip step #4. In any case, use stop loss to protect your investment.

#Filler: The Ten Commandments of Investing.
http://www.investopedia.com/articles/basics/07/10commandments.asp

●   Set goals. * Personal finances in order. * Ask questions. * Do not follow the herd. * Due diligence. * Be humble. * Be patient. * Be moderate. * No unnecessary churning. * Be safe. * Do not follow blindly.

Bonus: Investing for 'lazy' folks

You have better things to do than investing or you do not have the time, the desire to learn and/or expertise in investing. You should be better off to buy ETFs.

I recommend the following 4 ETFs. If you have $100,000 to invest, buy $25,000 for each recommended ETF. Consult your financial advisor before taking any action. The recommended ETFs should have a large market cap (the ETFs themselves and not the stocks they hold) and have a high volume.

Most returns started on July 1 and ended on July 1 the following year; this article is written on July 20, 2021. All are annualized returns for easy comparison. Fees, commissions and dividends have not been included; you can add the dividend yield and prorate it for YTD return.

Symbol	Name	YTD[1] Return	1 Year[2]	5 Years[3]	Bear[4]
IWF	Russel 1000G	30%	34%	40%	-33%
QQQ	QQQ	30%	46%	42%	-31%
VTI	Vang. Viper Tot	34%	22%	42%	-35%
VUG	Vang. Growth	37%	33%	41%	-32%
Avg.		31%	34%	41%	-33%
SPY[5]		34%	21%	39%	-35%
Beat[6]		-9%	60%	6%	7%

[1] The start date is 1/4/2021 and the end date is 7/1/2021.
[2] The start date is 7/1/2020 and the end date is 7/1/2021.
[3] The start date is 7/1/2016 and the end date is 7/1/2021.
[4] The start date is 1/2/2008 and the end date is 4/1/2009. My estimates.
[5] SPY is the ETF for the S&P 500 index. It is used as a yardstick.
[6] = (Avg. − SPY) / SPY. Again, it does not include fees, commissions and dividends.

Comments:

- The YTD is the only period that this portfolio does not beat SPY (the market to many). It could mean the market could be changing the favorite from growth stocks to value stocks. However, 31% return is far above the average of the market.

- The one-year return beats the market by 60%.
- The 5-year return beats SPY only by 6%, but the return of 41% is nothing to sneeze at.
- All except Vanguard's Viper Total are ETFs for growth stocks. Hence, I expected it would not beat the market, but it still did by 7%.
- You can time the market using the techniques described in this book as often as you can. When the indicator tells you to exit, you can sell these ETFs and reenter the market when it recovers. Riskier investors can buy contra ETFs such as PSQ and SH instead of holding cash when the market is down.
- At least once in a year review the selection. Use ETFdb.com for information. If you do not have time, it is fine skipping the review. When you switch ETFs, taxes should be considered.
- Most ETFs replace some stocks periodically to ensure better appreciation potential.

Bonus: Sample portfolio

It is a suggested sample. You need to tailor it to fit your personal requirements and your risk tolerance. In general, you should have an emergency fund for at least 3 months (6 months preferred). Many of our generation have one or even no layoff. However, I estimate the current generation will have 3 layoffs in their work life. It is due to automation, artificial intelligence, global economy, etc.

The rough estimate of stock holding in distribution between stock and bond is equal to 100 − Your Age. To illustrate in the following three portfolios, I use a 30-year-old, and hence he should have 70% in stocks and 30% in bonds (including gold, CDs and cash).

In addition, some sectors are better than others according to the market conditions. The following three portfolios are for regular, todays' market and one during a market crash. I use low-cost ETFs exclusively. ETF is exchange-traded funds. They are traded similar to stocks, but most are more diversified; their fees are usually lower than mutual funds.

ETF	Normal	Today (2/2021)	Crashing[5]
SPY[1]	40%	30%	0%
QQQ[2]	5%	10%	0%
ARKK[2]	5%	0%	0%
VTIAX[3]	20%	5%	0%
LQD[3]	15%	20%	5%
GLD	5%	15%	15%
CD	5%	0%	0%
Cash	5%	20%	60%[6]
SH[4]	0%	0%	5%
PSQ[4]	0%	0%	15%

[1] VOO is a low-fee alternative for SPY.

[2] QQQ has more tech stocks, while ARKK is an actively managed ETF specializing in 'disruptive technologies'. During market crashes, avoid them, esp. ARKK.

[3] VTIAX is an ETF for global companies. LQD is an ETF for corporate bonds.

[4] SH and PSQ are contra ETF to SPY and QQQ. They are shorting the corresponding index. When the market is recovering, switch them back to SPY and QQQ.

[5] Need to balance the allocations about two times a year as ETFs can grow or shrink. When the market crashes, rebalance it right away. All markets will crash, and the last two (2000 and 2008) have an average loss of about 45%. Refer to the chapter "Simplest marketing timing".

[6] Today's low interest rate does not benefit us for CDs. I would leave the cash not invested and wait for the recovery to move back to stocks.

Of course, everyone's situation is different. If you are conservative, do not buy SH and PSQ. If you are afraid of inflation (especially due to the excessive printing of money), allocate more on GLD, a gold ETF.

Do not listen to financial news. They are used by institutional investors / analysts to manipulate the market. Many times they act the opposite from what they preach. This is the primary reason retail investors do not do better. With the GameStop incident, do not invest in most hedge funds. Buffett has proved the hedge funds with their high fees cannot buy an indexed ETF such as SPY.

The above is my recommendation. In the long run, it should work fine. Consult your financial advisor before taking actions. Most info is from RainIsHere, a Cantonese YouTuber.

#Filler: Simple measures to reduce net security.
Do not click any links from unknown sources. Some seem to be ok but not.
MalwareBytes, for checking viruses, is free for download (they do not pay me).

Personally, I use a Chromebook for my financial transactions and a two-factor login for my stock trading.

#Filler Buffett, the person.
https://www.youtube.com/watch?v=w-eX4sZi-Zs

Book 7: Investing Strategies

An **investing strategy** is a structured approach for identifying, analyzing, buying, and selling stocks. Most strategies begin with stock screens or searches, followed by analysis and specific buy/sell criteria.

Types of Strategies
I classify strategies based on **holding period**:
- **Long-term strategies**: Holding periods of **one year or more**. These are typically **fundamentally based**—the market may take time to recognize the value.
  - Examples: *Redefined Dogs of the Dow*, year-end strategies, dividend investing.
- **Short-term strategies**: Holding periods of **one to three months**. These often rely on **momentum** and require quicker decisions.
  - Examples: *Momentum strategies*, *Sector Rotation*, *Insider Trading*.

There are also:
- **Swing trading**: Typically 2–6 months
- **Day trading**: Positions opened and closed within a single day
- **Shorting strategies**: Often around one month or less

⚠ *Using a long-term strategy for short-term trades, or vice versa, often leads to poor results. For taxable accounts, use long-term strategies for better long-term capital gain treatment.*

Risk and Strategy Fit
Each strategy can be categorized as **safer** or **riskier**. Choose one that aligns with your **risk tolerance** and **investment goals**. Market conditions also play a significant role—strategies that work in a bull market may underperform during a downturn.
For example:
- **Value stocks** tend to outperform during market bottoms.
- **Growth stocks and momentum strategies** do better during uptrends (the "Up Phase" in my market cycle model).

Practical Use and Testing
This book includes strategies and styles like:

- Swing Trading
- Sector Rotation
- Insider Trading
- Momentum Investing
- Penny and Micro Cap Stocks
- Dividend Investing
- Additional miscellaneous strategies

It's unlikely any individual can master them all. I've typically read two books per strategy and combined the key takeaways with my personal experiences. Some strategies I haven't fully tested—but they've been **proven successful by others** in specific market conditions.

Always match the strategy to the market environment.
Before committing real money:
- **Paper trade** (track simulated trades without using cash)
- **Backtest** strategies where possible using historical data
- Choose strategies that have recently performed well (e.g., over the last three months)
- Ensure it fits your personal risk profile

You can use spreadsheets or charting tools (like Yahoo! Finance or Finviz) to analyze performance of technical parameters. Keep in mind:
- Many online charts lack deep **fundamental metrics** like Debt/Equity ratios.
- Manual testing (updating weekly or monthly) takes time, but can be revealing
- Alternatively, use historical data together with Excel to test strategies like *Momentum* vs. *Sideways Trading*. Subscriptions to systems that have historical databases are available at a fee such as VectorVest — many have survivorship basis.

My Portfolio Allocation
You don't have to choose between being an investor or a trader—you can be both. Personally:
- **80%** of my portfolio is in **long-term investing**
- **20%** is in **short-term trading**
- This ratio adjusts depending on market conditions and your risk tolerance.

For beginners, I suggest starting with **long-term swing trading**:
- Focus on fundamentally sound stocks
- Review holdings every 6 months
- Sell if fundamentals deteriorate

Brief Critique of Popular Strategies

Each strategy has its strengths—but also important **limitations**. Here are some quick cautions:
- **Sector Rotation**
  - ➤ Requires ongoing research and quick adjustments; sector trends can reverse abruptly.
- **Insider Trading**
  - ➤ Don't treat insider buys as pure value indicators—sometimes insiders are wrong. Use this as a **momentum** signal, not a value one.
- **Penny & Micro-Cap Stocks**
  - ➤ I prefer **micro-caps** (slightly larger, more liquid). Avoid stocks with insufficient volume—ensure the **daily volume is at least 10x your planned buy size**.
- **Momentum**
  - ➤ Don't overstay—momentum can **reverse quickly**. Exit as soon as strength fades.
- **Dividend Strategies**
  - ➤ Don't chase high yields blindly. Dividends are appealing when bond yields are low, but rising interest rates can reduce their appeal and stock prices.

Final Thoughts

The **average return** of each strategy varies depending on screen parameters, market cycle, and investor behavior. Use average returns as rough guidance only.
- **Stick with a winning strategy** until its performance declines.
- If a strategy underperforms, **analyze what went wrong**—and go back to paper trading until you rebuild confidence.

Investing isn't about mastering every strategy—it's about understanding which one suits **you**, the **market**, and the **moment**.

Overview of an Investing Strategy (by ChatGPT)

An effective investing strategy is a systematic plan that guides how you allocate capital, manage risk, and pursue returns over time. While details vary by individual goals and risk tolerance, every robust strategy shares these core components:

1. Define Your Objectives
- **Time Horizon:** Are you saving for retirement in 30 years, a home purchase in five, or a shorter-term goal?
- **Return Target:** Do you aim to match inflation, beat the market by a certain percentage, or generate steady income?
- **Risk Tolerance:** How much volatility can you stomach—both financially and emotionally?

2. Asset Allocation
Divide your portfolio among broad asset classes based on your objectives and risk profile:
- **Equities (Stocks):** Growth potential but higher volatility.
- **Fixed Income (Bonds, CDs):** Income generation with lower expected returns and reduced swings.
- **Alternatives (Real Estate, Commodities, REITs):** Diversification benefits and inflation hedges.
- **Cash & Cash Equivalents:** Liquidity cushion and capital preservation.

A classic guideline is **"100 minus your age"** in equities, but modern variations factor in risk tolerance and market conditions.

3. Diversification
Within each asset class, spread your investments to avoid concentration risk:
- **Global Exposure:** U.S., developed international, and emerging markets.
- **Sector Balance:** Technology, healthcare, financials, consumer staples, etc.
- **Market Capitalization:** Large-cap stability vs. small-cap growth potential.

4. Security Selection
Choose specific investments—individual stocks, bonds, or funds—using criteria such as:
- **Fundamentals:** Earnings growth, valuation multiples (P/E, P/B), balance-sheet strength.
- **Income Metrics:** Dividend yield and payout ratio for income-oriented portfolios.
- **Technical Factors:** Trend confirmation (e.g., moving averages), relative strength.

- **Analyst & Quant Scores:** Consensus ratings, proprietary composite scores.

Many investors lean on low-cost **index ETFs** to capture broad market returns with minimal selection bias.

5. Entry & Exit Rules

- **Dollar-Cost Averaging:** Invest a fixed amount periodically to smooth out market timing.
- **Value Averaging:** Adjust contributions based on target portfolio value.
- **Stop-Loss Orders:** Predefine a maximum acceptable loss to limit downside.
- **Profit Targets & Rebalancing:** Trim winners that exceed target allocations; top up underperformers to maintain your desired mix.

6. Risk Management

- **Position Sizing:** Limit any single holding to a small percentage (e.g., 3–5%) of portfolio value.
- **Hedging:** Use inverse ETFs or options to protect against broad market declines.
- **Cash Reserves:** Keep an emergency fund equal to 3–6 months of living expenses.

7. Monitoring & Review

- **Regular Check-Ins:** Quarterly or semiannual reviews to track performance and rebalance.
- **Performance Attribution:** Identify which assets, sectors, or strategies drove returns.
- **Strategy Adjustments:** Adapt asset allocation or selection criteria to evolving goals, market conditions, or life events.

8. Behavioral Discipline

- **Stay the Course:** Avoid emotional reactions to market noise.
- **Maintain a Plan:** Only deviate from your strategy when you've conducted a structured review—not on impulse.
- **Continuous Learning:** Stay informed about economic trends, new tools (like AI stock screeners), and evolving best practices.

Bottom Line: A clear, repeatable framework—grounded in defined objectives, diversified allocations, disciplined rules, and regular reviews—anchors successful investing. By combining sound research with steadfast execution, you give yourself the best chance to meet your financial goals over the long term.

1   Introduction

A trading strategy is a systematic approach to identifying, analyzing, buying, and selling stocks, often using screens or searches. This guide focuses on screening for stocks, with an emphasis on value investing, though other strategies like momentum are also discussed.

Key Insights
- **No Evergreen Strategies**: Market conditions change, and so should your strategies. What worked in the past may not work today.
- **Market Cycles Matter**: Different strategies perform better in different phases (e.g., value stocks during recovery, momentum stocks in bullish markets).
- **Testing is Crucial**: Regularly test strategies using historical data to ensure they align with current market conditions.
- **Discipline is Key**: Stick to your strategy, use stop-loss orders, and adjust trailing stops for appreciated trades.

A Sample Strategy

Three-Step Process
1. **When to Search**: Conduct searches monthly or when market risk is low.
2. **What to Buy**: Use fundamental analysis to filter stocks (details below).
3. **When to Sell**: Exit positions when the market plunges, objectives are met, or stocks no longer meet criteria.

Fundamental Analysis Criteria
- **Listing**: Stocks must be listed on major U.S. exchanges (no ADRs or partnerships unless specialized).
- **Market Cap**: Over $100M (or $10B for blue chips).
- **Price**: Above $2.
- **Liquidity**: Average daily volume at least 20x your potential position.
- **Valuation**:
    - P/E < 20 with positive earnings.
    - P/Cash Flow < 25 with positive cash flow.
    - Debt/Equity < 1 (preferably 0.5, industry-dependent).
- **Quality**:

- o Fidelity's Equity Summary Score ≥ 7.
- o Piotroski (if you have this parameter) F-Score ≥ 7.

Testing strategies

Tools for Backtesting
- Free screeners: Finviz.com, broker platforms (limited historical data).
- Paid services: VectorVest, Zacks, Portfolio123 (offer historical data for robust testing).

Key Considerations
1. **Survivorship Bias**: Ensure databases include delisted or bankrupt stocks to avoid inflated results.
2. **Time Periods**: Test across multiple market cycles (e.g., 2000–2019) and phases (bullish, bearish, recovery).
3. **Benchmarking**: Compare returns to relevant benchmarks (e.g., S&P 500, sector-specific ETFs).
4. **Holding Periods**:
   - o Value strategies: 6+ months.
   - o Momentum strategies: 1–3 months.
5. **Risk Metrics**: Evaluate maximum drawdown, Sharpe ratio, and win rate.

Testing Workflow
1. Define parameters (e.g., market cap, P/E).
2. Sort and select top stocks (e.g., by Earnings Yield).
3. Simulate performance over varying holding periods.
4. Compare results to benchmarks and adjust criteria as needed.

Monitoring and Execution
Performance Tracking
- Maintain watchlists (e.g., "YearEnd 20211215") to track screened stocks.
- Compare performance to benchmarks (e.g., SPY) over 1–6 months.

Execution Tips
- **Discipline**: Follow your trade plan strictly.
- **Buy in Uptrends**: Use SMA-20, SMA-50, and SMA-200 to confirm trends.
- **Narrow Selections**: Focus on top 5 stocks or tighten criteria if too many options arise.
- **Emotion Management**: Avoid deviations from tested strategies.

Pitfalls and Adjustments

Common Issues

- **Survivorship Bias**: Overestimating returns by ignoring failed stocks.
- **Emotional Trading**: Straying from the strategy due to fear or greed.
- **Market Changes**: Strategies may underperform in current conditions.

Solutions

- Regularly update tests using recent data (last 6 months).
- Diversify strategies to adapt to market phases.
- Use stop-loss orders to limit drawdowns.

Conclusion

Successful stock trading requires a dynamic, tested approach tailored to market conditions. By combining rigorous screening, disciplined execution, and continuous monitoring, investors can improve their odds of outperforming the market. Remember: no strategy works forever— stay adaptable and always test before committing real capital.

Links:

Fidelity Trading Strategies:
https://www.fidelity.com/learning-center/trading/types-of-trading-strategies/overview

Top swing pattern:
https://www.youtube.com/watch?v=wH8GnsjoFb0

Understanding Maximum Drawdown
Sharpe Ratio Explained

#Filler: lessons from a strategy named Turtle with my inputs

The experiment to train students who have no experience in two weeks worked. The technical analysis strategy would not work today for many reasons. However, the concepts are still good and explained here.

Do not time the market (not agree totally). Find a good strategy (easier said than done) and stick with it consistently. Cash management (agree with stops from 5% to 15% depending on your risk tolerance and the volatility of the stocks). Do not use leverage that could wipe out your entire portfolio. Follow the trend of the stock with higher positions.

Monitor strategy performance

Key Principles
- **Stay Current**: Regularly assess recent performance to avoid outdated strategies.
- **Survivorship Bias Alert**: Ensure backtesting includes delisted or bankrupt stocks for accurate results.
- **Benchmark Reliably**: Compare returns to relevant indices (e.g., SPY for broad market, Russell 2000 for small caps).

Practical Steps
1. **Create Watchlists**:
   - Example: "YearEnd_20211215" tracks stocks screened on 12/15/2021.
   - Compare performance against SPY over 1–6 months.
2. **Use Tools**: Leverage Finviz or Fidelity for analysis; manually track prices in spreadsheets if needed.
3. **Test Metrics**: Evaluate individual factors (e.g., P/E) to identify drivers of performance.

Executing Strategies with Discipline

Best Practices
- **Follow Your Plan**: Adhere strictly to predefined rules (entry/exit criteria, position sizing).
- **Buy in Uptrends**: Confirm trends using SMA-20, SMA-50, and SMA-200 alignment.
- **Narrow Selections**:
  - Focus on top 5 stocks (e.g., high E/P for value, strong SMA-50 for momentum).
  - Eliminate outliers (e.g., high debt-to-equity stocks).

Managing Challenges
- **No Stocks Found?** Relax criteria or skip the cycle.
- **Max Drawdown Awareness**: Set stop-loss orders based on tested risk limits (e.g., 15% loss cap for volatile strategies).

Advanced Strategy Insights
Leveraging Historical Data
- **Proven Metrics**: Prioritize research-backed parameters (e.g., Piotroski F-Score, EV/EBITDA).
- **Tailor Tests**:
  - Short-term strategies: Test 1–3 month holds.
  - Long-term strategies: Evaluate over 6–18 months.
- **Window Testing**: Simulate rolling periods (e.g., Jan 2000–Jan 2001, Feb 2000–Feb 2001) to smooth outliers.

Pitfalls & Solutions

Issue	Solution
Survivorship Bias	Use databases that retain delisted stocks or manually account for failures.
Emotional Trading	Automate trades or set predefined rules to minimize interference.
Idle Cash Between Trades	Allocate unused funds to low-risk ETFs (e.g., SPY) during downtime.

Performance Metrics
- **Sharpe Ratio**: Assess risk-adjusted returns (>1 is ideal).
- **Win Rate**: Aim for ≥55% with balanced risk/reward.
- **Market Cycle Adaptation**: Rotate strategies (e.g., growth stocks in bull markets, defensive stocks in downturns).

Key Takeaways
1. **Test Rigorously**: Backtest across multiple cycles and adjust for biases.
2. **Execute Calmly**: Stick to your plan—avoid emotional decisions.
3. **Adapt Continuously**: Update strategies based on recent performance and market phases.
   "The market rewards flexibility. Your strategy should evolve as the data does."

Filler: Max. drawdown.

'Max. drawdown' should be understood for short-term investors. It is the maximum money you can lose. If your tested strategy tells you that you can lose 40% in this strategy, then you should place the stops accordingly. To illustrate, you bought MSFT for $100, and it dipped to $50, your max. drawdown is $50 or 50%. If you use margin, your broker would issue a margin call on its way to the $50 drop. Eventually the stock would recover and hit the $200 mark, and the long-term holders are glad that they did not close the position.

Filler: An Offensive Joke (to some)

Outside a Catholic college, there was a large sign that read: *"Escort Service Available After Dark."*

Curious—and hopeful—my friend (not me) called the number, expecting the kind of "escort service" you'd find in the Yellow Pages.

Let's just say... he was *not* expecting a campus security escort to the parking lot. He's still upset about the "false advertising."

Section I: Common strategy ideas

2   Screening stocks

A screen is part of a strategy to find potential stocks to buy. It limits the number of stocks to evaluate. Evaluate the screened stocks to find the better ones. Buy them for the right prices. Set the exit procedure such as losing 12% or making over 25%. The optimal performance of holding the stock is 6 months for the Insider strategy for example. When you have the stock for 6 months, do another evaluation to determine your buy/hold decision. Monitor your performance.

It works for me with about 40 screens. I check out the recent performances periodically and select the top screens (about 4 usually).

Before looking for stocks, check out whether the market is risky. After screening, I score the screened stocks and do some further evaluation before I purchase any stock.

When we follow all the above, there is still no guarantee that we'll make money. In the long run, we do and it is far better to follow a proven strategy than not to.

Here are some free sites for screens.

More description: article
http://stocks.about.com/od/researchtools/a/071909screenlist.htm

Swing trading: https://www.youtube.com/watch?v=ldDsi8F4ZeA

#Filler: Simple measures to reduce net security.
Do not click any links from unknown sources. Some seems to be ok but not.

"MalwareBytes", for checking viruses, is free for download (they do not pay me).

Personally, I use a Chromebook for my financial transactions and a two-factor logon for my stock trading.

A simple tutorial

This tutorial is for beginners using Finviz's Screener to screen value stocks of large companies with my own preferences. Bring up Finviz, and select Screener, which has 3 sections: Descriptive, Fundamental and Technical.

- **Index.** S&P 500.
- **Country.** USA (my personal reference).

Select the second section (Fundamental).
- **Forward P/E.** Under 25. I prefer under 15 for non-tech stocks.
- **Price/Free Cash Flow.** Under 25. This metric had been ignored by many.
- **Debt / Equity.** Under 1.

Select the last section (Technical)
- **200-Day SMA.** Above SMA200.

The number of screen stocks is still too many for individual evaluation. Ignore the stocks Insiders are dumping (more than negative 10% for me). Ignore all stocks with negative earnings (i.e., Forward P/E = '-'). You can sort Forward P/E in ascending order and evaluate the first 10 stocks (or more depending how much time you have).

Alternatively, add the following to reduce the number to the one you desire: RSI(14) (less than 50 for example), Return of Equity (more than 15 for example) and EPS Growth Qtr over Qtr (over 5% or example).

You can save this screen for future use. Evaluate each screened stock. Start with Fidelity's Equity Summary Score (prefer over 7) and Yahoo!Finance's (under Statistics) Enterprise Value / EBITDA (EBITDA/ Enterprise Value should be over 5%).

As in most screeners, this one has many limitations. The number of limitations has been reduced with the paid subscription. Many can be resolved by using multiple screens such as different Market Cap and higher debt for some sectors.

Screening momentum stocks uses different metrics such as high 50-SMA.

Since Finviz does not have a historical database for fundamental metrics, you cannot test how your screen performs. Save the evaluated stocks in a watch list and update the performance periodically (a year for value screens and 1 to 3 months for momentum screens).

Buy the stock and set your exit policy to complete the strategy.

3 Experiences and lessons in strategies

The Strategy-Market Fit
- **Dynamic Alignment**: No strategy works universally—match approaches to current market conditions (bull, bear, or sideways).
- **Emotional Discipline**: Separate decisions from market noise; stick to predefined rules.

"A perfect strategy-market fit is rare—but when it happens, the rewards are explosive."

Proven Strategies in Action

1. Sideways Markets (e.g., 2015)
Tactic: Buy dips, sell temporary highs.
- **Entry Signals:**
  - 2% drop from prior session **or** 5% below 5-day high.
- **Exit Signals:**
  - 2% gain from prior session **or** 5% above 5-day low.
- **Tools**: Use ETFs like SPY/IWM for liquidity; hold 1 day–2 weeks.
- **Risk Control**: Hard stops at 15% loss.

Example:
- Buy SPY at $390 (5% below 5-day high of $410).
- Sell at $400 (2% above purchase).

2. Trending Markets

Market Phase	Strategy	Holding Period	Key Metric
Bull	Momentum ("Buy high, sell higher")	1–3 months	SMA-50 crossover
Bear	Contra ETFs	1 month	Downward SMA-200

Caution: Momentum fails in high volatility—switch to value or cash.

3. Value Investing
- **Holding Period**: 1+ years (wait for market recognition).
- **Screen For:**

- o   Low P/E (<20), strong cash flow, manageable debt (D/E <0.5).
- **Case Study**:
  - o   SMCI: Sold at 300% profit (missed 1,200% due to emotional exit—highlighting the need for trailing stops).

Advanced Tactics
Special Situations

Strategy	Catalyst	Example
Turnarounds	Operational fixes (e.g., cost cuts)	ALU (2013): Patents > Debt
Breakups	Sum-of-parts valuation	Recent tech spin-offs
Insider Buys	Executives investing heavily	Filter for non-routine buys

Market-Neutral & Sector Strategies
- **Market-Neutral**: Pair long/short stocks to hedge market risk.
- **Sector Rotation**: Shift into uptrending sectors (e.g., tech in recoveries, staples in recessions).
- **Theme Investing**: ETFs like FXI (China), GLD (gold) for macro trends.

Critical Lessons
Common Pitfalls
- **Early Exits**: Selling winners too soon (e.g., GameStop, TTWO held since 2015 at 50% annualized).
- **Misaligned Timing**: Value investing during momentum rallies.
- **Overconfidence**: Leveraging home equity in 2009 (risky!).

Post-Trade Reflections
- **"Buy & Monitor"**: Adapt "buy & hold" with periodic reviews (e.g., avoid dying industries like print media). With the internet, many newspapers such as Washington Post suffer financially, so are their stock prices. The other example is the retail sector when Amazon.com takes over.

- **"Buy & Forget"**: For deep-value stocks in recoveries (e.g., MSFT/CAT in 2012).

Execution Checklist
1. **Test First**: Backtest strategies (e.g., 2000–2019 cycles).
2. **Match Conditions**: Use:
   - Momentum in bulls.
   - Value in recoveries.
   - Swing trades in sideways markets.
3. **Set Rules**: Define entries, exits, and stops upfront.

"The market rewards those who plan more than those who panic."

Links:

- Sector Rotation Guide:
  http://en.wikipedia.org/wiki/Sector_rotation

- Market-Neutral Investing
  http://en.wikipedia.org/wiki/Sector_rotation

Filler: "First" as of 4/2016
This time could make some history at least for one of the following:
1. First woman president.
2. First spouse stays in the white house two times. "Buy one get one free" or give Bill another chance with the interns.
3. First non-politician president.
4. First president spending less in campaign.

So far, they try to satisfy every group (such as the Great Wall of the US, free tuition...) without telling us how to finance them.

4   *The best strategies*

Note. Most parameters described here such as SMA-20 and Short% can be found from Finviz.com

The #1 Strategy: Buy Low, Sell High (And Why Most Fail)
Core Principles
- **Contrarian Edge**:
    o Buy when others panic (e.g., Early Recovery phases like 2003/2009).
    o Sell when euphoria peaks (e.g., mother-in-law giving stock tips).
- **Valuation Focus**:
    o Target low P/E stocks (P/E <20) with positive earnings.
    o Avoid "falling knives"—only buy when root problems are fixed.

Key Signals

Action	Trigger	Example
SELL	Fed rates >5% + retail investor frenzy	Tech stocks in 2000
BUY	350-day SMA reversal + 2 years post-crash	Financials in 2009
AVOID	Sector winning streak >2 years	Dividend stocks in 2015

Case Study: Citigroup (C)
- 2008: Avoided at $550 (pre-crash bubble).
- 2009: Accumulated at $32 (P/E 9, post-plunge).
- 2019: $62 (+94% return).

Strategy #2: Buy High, Sell Higher (Momentum Mastery)
Rules for Riding Trends
1. **Entry**: Price >50-day SMA (Finviz.com).
2. **Exit**:
    o Price <SMA OR RSI(14) >70 (overbought).
    o Partial sells at 10-15% stops (adjust for volatility).

3. **Sweet Spot**: Large caps ($1B-5B market cap) with 3x average volume.

When to Avoid:
- Risky markets (SMA-200 declining).
- Speculative small-caps ($100M-500M)—prone to manipulation.

Strategy #3: Buy Very High, Sell Even Higher (Bubble Surfing)
High-Risk, High-Reward Tactics
- **Targets**:
  - Stocks breaking 52-week highs + institutional interest.
  - Sector ETFs with SMA200% >0 (uptrend confirmation).
- **Management**:
  - Daily monitoring (watch RSI(14) >65).
  - Mental trailing stops (e.g., 20% below peak).
- **Golden Rule**: Never short these—ride the wave or stay out.

The "Buy & Monitor" Hybrid Strategy
Long-Term Winners Checklist
Hold Criteria:
- Fundamentals: Forward P/E 5-25, Debt/Equity <0.25, ROE >15%.
- Technicals: RSI(14) <35, SMA200% >0.
- Growth: Sales Q/Q >15%, EPS Q/Q >10%.

Sell Triggers:
- Industry disruption (e.g., Circuit City vs. Amazon).
- Legal risks or R&D cuts (for growth stocks).

Performance Proof:

Stock	Holding Period	Total Return	Annualized
TTWO	2015-2018	377%	124%
STX	2015-2018	88%	29%
VS SPY	Same Period	29%	10%

Pro Tips for All Strategies
1. **Tax Efficiency**:

- ○ Gift appreciated stocks to family (reset cost basis).
- ○ Roth accounts for dividend stocks (avoid income tax).

2. **Sector Rotation:**
   - ○ Tech in recoveries → Staples in recessions.
3. **Toolkit:**
   - ○ Finviz.com (screeners), SMA/RSI charts (trend confirmation).

"The market rewards patience in value plays and speed in momentum trades—but punishes stubbornness in both."
Resources

My long-term grade

Forward P/E (5 to 25), low Debt/Equity (less than .25), high Cash/Share, larger Market Cap (> 200M), high ROE (>15%), low RSI(14) (less than 35), high Insider Own/Purchase, Sales Q/Q (>15%), EPS Q/Q (>10%) and SMA200% (>0). In addition, they have competitive products, invest heavily in research (except for established companies), and there are no serious lawsuits pending.

#Filler: Depending Who You Talk To

Say "White lives matter" as a white guy, and it's labeled offensive.
Say "Black lives matter" as a black guy, and it's a movement.
Same with phrases like "white power," "black power," or even "yellow power."

The meaning changes depending on *who* says it—sometimes more than *what* is actually said.

Context isn't just everything—it's the *only* thing.

Filler: Lifetime Guarantee
Eat more veggies, skip the fried meats, exercise regularly, avoid alcohol, smoking, and definitely no buffets.

Follow all that, and I guarantee you'll live two years longer.
It's a lifetime guarantee...
Of course, it's *your* life—not mine.

5   Different investment styles

There are three major styles to evaluate stocks: Fundamental, Growth and Technical Analysis (TA).

The debate on their benefits could be endless. I believe TA is good for short term (1 month for stocks), growth for intermediate term (say 3 months) and fundamental is good for longer term (say 6 months). Here is my summary of the two (I place Fundamental and Growth into the same group for discussion here).   Market sometimes favors value (i.e., fundamentals) and sometimes growth.

TA depends mostly on the stock price and hence it predicts the trend better; it also can track oversold conditions. TA would catch the stock movement, but not by fundamental or growth metrics.

- TA.
  Most TAers (those who practice technical analysis) do not care about fundamentals, but price and volume. They do have good arguments. A lot of data about the stock are not available or too late to be effective such as a new drug discovery, being acquired, or a serious lawsuit pending.

  The following are two illustrations on how TAers can benefit.

  When the insiders and/or analysts know about some promising new products or positive unexpected earnings, they buy and tell their families to buy. I do not judge whether it is Illegal insider trading or not. TAers notice the rise of the stock price with increasing volume and they buy. Many times, the last ones to buy may end up losing money as the insiders would unload them especially when the stock prices are overvalued.

  When the institutional investors (pension fund managers and fund managers) are buying a specific stock, the stock volume and its price will both rise. TAers would notice them from the charts and jump on the bandwagon. To me, this is the basic reason on how good day traders make money. It usually takes a week for an institutional investor to finish trading a stock.

  'Max. drawdown' should be understood for short-term investors. It is the maximum money you can lose. If your tested strategy tells you that you can lose 40% in this strategy, then you should place the stops accordingly. To illustrate, you bought MSFT for $100, and it dipped to $50, your max. drawdown is $50 or 50%. If you use margin, your broker would issue a margin call on its way to the $50 drop. Eventually the stock would recover and hit the $200 mark, and the long-term holders are glad that they did not close the position.

- Fundamentals.
  They look at the companies' metrics such as P/E, expected P/E, PEG, debt, sales growth, etc. A good company's stock price with rising profit and rising sales should appreciate in the long term. Some short the stocks of companies with bad fundamentals. In some cases, data is hidden in the financial statements that most metrics do not detect.

To conclude, the best TAers and the best fundamentalists usually make money in either market in the long run. However, fundamental analysis is easier to master and they have made more money than TAers in the long run. You find a lot of successful fundamentalists from Buffett and his followers, but not too many successful TAers. Some successful TAers even lose their accumulated fortunes. Be warned that if you do not know what you're doing in either discipline, you will lose money. Learn it and trade it on paper before committing even small amounts of real money   to   it.

The best way is using both disciplines in selecting stocks as described below.

- When your chart(s) displays a candidate to buy, take a look at the fundamentals. If the fundamentals are bad, be cautious. Some screens can search for the stocks with good technical patterns (Finviz.com is one).

- After you spot a bargain stock to buy via the fundamental metrics, check out its SMA-200 (Simple Moving Average for the last 200 trade sessions) or any duration that fits your purpose. If the price is above the moving average, it could be a buy.

Afterthoughts

- Try the following to see whether fundamental works better if you have a historical database.

Fundamentals

1. Include all stocks that are below the 200-day SMA (Simple Moving Average) - opposite of what a TAer would do.
2. The expected positive P/Es have to be between 4 and 15. In addition, both profits and sales are rising by 5%.
3. Exclude financial companies like banks and insurance, miners, bio companies and drug companies that are hard to evaluate.

TA

1. Buy stocks that cross over the 50-day, simple moving averages.
2. Never buy stocks when the market is below 200-day, simple moving average.

Check the result in 1-month intervals and 6 months intervals. My own simple test favors the fundamentals in 6 months intervals and favors TA in 1-month intervals. You may need more exhaustive testing to draw a good conclusion in different phases of a market cycle for at least 2 market cycles.

- SMA-200 (from Finviz.com without charts) and its variations are the ones most TAers use and even most experienced fundamentalists know how to use it if they want to. It is also a good indicator for the general market by using an ETF that simulates the market.
  There are many sophisticated TA indicators in Yahoo!Finance. For qualified clients, Fidelity provides a tool to backtest your TA strategies.
- It may be beneficial to use fundamentals to look for stocks and use TA to find the entry and exit points. Today's screens can do it in the reverse order, or both in the same screen.

- Fundamentals can be divided into Value and Growth.
  Value. I use it mostly. Especially good in the early recovery phase of the market cycle.

6   Mastering Market Timing for Value Opportunities

The Early Recovery Sweet Spot

Value investing shines brightest during market recoveries. My 80% returns in 2009 weren't accidental - they capitalized on the Early Recovery phase when:

- P/Es remain elevated but PEG ratios begin improving
- Quality companies trade at crisis prices despite sound fundamentals
- Market sentiment shifts from panic to cautious optimism

Pro Tip: Track the 350-day SMA - when markets cross above this threshold after a 20%+ decline, the Early Recovery phase typically begins.

Identifying True Value vs. Value Traps

Screening Criteria for Crisis Markets

Metric	Ideal Target	Red Flags
Cash Runway	>24 months	<12 months
EV/EBITDA	<8x sector average	Negative
Insider Activity	Net buying	Heavy selling
Price/Cash	<1.0x	N/A (qualitative)

Case Study: December 2018

- Scored 50%+ returns in one month by targeting:
  - Stocks down 50%+ but still profitable
  - Strong balance sheets (cash > short-term liabilities)
  - Positive free cash flow

The Value Investor's Toolbox
Essential Valuation Metrics

1. **EV/EBITDA** (Yahoo Finance): Superior to P/E as it accounts for debt
2. **FCF/Share** (Finviz): Reveals true cash generation
3. **Insider Transactions** (SEC Form 4 filings): Follow the smart money

Modern Adjustments:
- For tech: Raise P/E ceiling to 25
- For biotech: Focus on cash runway over earnings
- For turnarounds: Require SMA-50 confirmation

Executing the Strategy
Three-Phase Approach
1. **Identification**:
   o Screen for Price/Cash <1 (Finviz)
   o Filter out "zombie" companies in dying industries
   o Verify with Fidelity Equity Score ≥7
2. **Validation**:
   o Check 2-year cash runway (10-Q/K filings)
   o Research litigation risks (PACER)
   o Confirm insider confidence
3. **Timing**:
   o Enter when SMA-20 turns positive
   o Scale in over 3-6 months
   o Set 25% trailing stops

Portfolio Tip: Allocate 3-5% per position - even Buffett misses sometimes (see: IBM)
Avoiding Common Pitfalls
The Value Trap Checklist
- Declining ROIC 3 years running
- Dividend payout >120% of FCF
- Negative earnings revisions
- Sector disruption risk (e.g., BBBY vs. Amazon)

When to Pass:
- Complex financials (banks, insurers)
- Binary outcome stocks (biotech trials)
- "Story" stocks without tangible metrics

"Be greedy when others are fearful, but verify before you buy." - Modern interpretation of Buffett

This approach combines traditional value principles with modern market dynamics, emphasizing rigorous due diligence and disciplined entry/exit strategies. The key is patience - true value realization often takes 12-24 months.

A good Link: Peter Lynch:
https://www.youtube.com/watch?v=J1DFMXL2kXE&t=2304s
I have proven market timing worked fine in the 2000 and 2008 market crashes. I bought many products from BBB, and they are close to bankruptcy. Buffett was late in buying Apple, as he did not use a smartphone. New drugs may not be understood by most investors and they could lose some buying opportunities. Hence, they have many exceptions.

7 AAII, a source for strategies

AAII's screens perform differently throughout economic phases. Here's how to align them:

Market Phase	Best Performing Screens	Key Indicators	Holding Period
Early Recovery	Deep Value	Low P/B, High FCF Yield	12-24 months
Bull Market	Growth Momentum	EPS Growth >25%, RS Rating >90	3-6 months
Market Peak	Dividend Aristocrats	Payout Ratio <75%, Yield >3%	6-12 months
Bear Market	Cash Position	Net Cash > Market Cap	Until recovery

Pro Tip: Combine AAII's "Shadow Stock" screen with SMA-200 timing for 32% better returns during recoveries (backtested 2009-2020).

Smart Implementation Strategies
Overcoming the 15-Day Lag
1. **Forward-Test**: Paper trade screens for 45 days before live implementation
2. **Sector Rotation**: Apply screens to currently leading sectors (use AAII's Sector Reports)

3. **Hybrid Approach**: Pair AAII fundamentals with your own technical triggers

Tax-Efficient Method:

- Use screens in Roth IRAs to avoid capital gains from high turnover
- For taxable accounts, modify rebalance frequency to quarterly

Performance Analysis Insights

Critical Lessons from AAII Data (2011-2016)

1. **The Winner's Curse**:
   - 2015's top screen ("Price-to-Free-Cash-Flow") underperformed SPY by 18% in 2016
   - Solution: Rotate to contrarian screens after strong outperformance

2. **Bear Market Reality**:
   - No AAII screen beat cash during 2008 (-37% average)
   - Must-use exit signal: Death Cross (50-day under 200-day SMA)

3. **The 5-Year Myth**:
   - Only 3 of 67 screens consistently beat SPY from 2011-2015
   - Outperformers shared: Low EV/EBITDA + Positive Insider Buying

Modern Optimization Tactics

Enhancing AAII Screens in 2024

1. **Add Filters**:
   - Exclude stocks under $5 billion during bear markets
   - Require SMA-50 > SMA-200 for momentum plays
2. **Synthetic Screen Creation**: Blend top-performing AAII factors: (PEG < 1.2) & (FCF_Yield > 8%) & (InsiderBuy_3Mo > InsiderSell_3Mo)
3. **Turnover Reduction**:
   - Modify monthly rebalancing to:
     - 25% position refresh monthly
     - Full rebalance only quarterly

Resource Tip: AAII's "Stock Investing Guide" provides backtesting templates to validate custom screens.

The Bottom Line

While AAII screens offer excellent starting points, their true power comes from:

1. **Cycle-Aware Implementation**: Match screens to current market phase
2. **Disciplined Timing**: Use technical indicators to override buy/sell signals
3. **Customization**: Adapt base screens to your risk parameters

"The screens are maps, but you're the navigator - adjust course for market weather conditions."

For current performance data and screen specifics, visit AAII's Screen Hub. Always paper trade new screens through at least one full market cycle (typically 3-5 years) before committing capital.

8   Profit from a proven strategy

This chapter explains how to make the most of a subscription-based stock-picking service—and even improve its results. We'll use AAII's Shadow Stock screen as an example, but these principles apply to most subscription services.

Does it perform?

According to AAII's own data, the Shadow Stock strategy has historically performed well. However, it experienced weaker returns in the period up to January 2016. It's important to note that the strategy uses real cash, so there's no theoretical back-test bias—but you should still be mindful of the following points:

- **Focus on the last 10 years of results.**
  Don't rely on very long-term performance data alone. Markets have changed dramatically in the past decade, so older returns aren't as predictive as recent ones.
- **Check if you can realistically match the published performance.**
  If the stock picks are distributed to other subscribers before you receive them, your results may differ. This isn't specific to AAII—it's a general risk with all such services.

First, verify that insiders at the service don't trade ahead of subscribers. Some services enforce rules to prevent this. Also, see if you have to pay extra to get the picks earlier than other members. Be wary: many self-styled gurus have poor track records. Searching for reviews of their past performance can save you money.

- **Consider doing your own stock selection.**
  Ideally, the service should give you the tools and data to choose stocks yourself, avoiding many pitfalls (especially with low-volume stocks). This approach takes more effort but can be more reliable.
- **Paying for extra data access.**
  Many services sell databases and screening tools separately. This can be worth it if it gives you an edge over the broader subscriber base—since a large group acting on the same picks can push prices up temporarily.

One effective tactic is to modify the recommended screens so they don't produce exactly the same stock lists as everyone else.

Once you have the selection list, analyze the stocks and test them with paper trading. If they outperform the market in both rising and falling environments, the service likely has real value.

Improving Performance

You can enhance results further by applying principles from this book:

- **Market timing by cycle.**
  Exit all positions before and during anticipated market plunges. Of course, you'll need to detect these downturns reliably to benefit.
- **Market timing by calendar.**
  For example, hold stocks from November 1 to May 1 in non-taxable accounts, as historical statistics often favor this period.
- **Diversification.**
  Avoid concentrating more than 25% of your portfolio in a single sector.
- **Skip complex sectors unless you have expertise.**
  Areas like banking, insurance, mining, and pharmaceuticals often require specialized knowledge.
- **Apply additional criteria.**
  Consider limiting yourself to large-cap stocks or other filters that may not be part of the service's default screen.
- **Modify the strategy.**
  Avoid trading the exact same stocks as everyone else. Herd behavior typically benefits those who move first. Adjust your filters so you're not merely following the crowd.

Subscription strategies often recommend selling any stock that no longer meets their criteria. To avoid selling late along with everyone else, you can add your own exit rules:

1. Sell *before* the herd. For instance, if the service suggests reviewing positions every 6 months, consider doing so at 5 months.
2. Modify selection criteria. If the service screens for market caps under $150 million, experiment with $100–300 million (as an example).

Analyzing and Trading Stocks

- **Analyze the stock.**
  Don't rely blindly on the screen. Look at fundamentals, technicals, and your own criteria.
- **Get a second opinion.**
  - Use resources like Fidelity. Only consider stocks with an Equity Summary Score of 8 or higher.
  - For value screens, plan to hold at least 6 months, focusing on fundamentals such as P/E ratios.
  - For momentum screens, limit holding periods to a month or less, using signals like moving averages or other technical metrics.
- **Buy the stock.**
- **Sell the stock.**
  Re-evaluate continually. If the stock meets your price target or its fundamentals decline, exit your position.

Links
Gurus are not gurus: https://www.cbsnews.com/news/who-are-the-most-least-accurate-stock-gurus/

#Filler: The other side of a story
The security guard slams the child in a mall or in a school all the time. The other side of the story is the bad behavior of today's children. The retail stores have to protect themselves as shoplifting by teenagers is quite common. Where were the parents? Education starts at home.

#Filler: How Short-Sellers "Steal" from You

Short-sellers can manipulate sentiment by spreading negative rumors—driving your stops and pocketing the gains. If you suspect foul play, sell at market price rather than triggering a stop. And remember: if the "too-good-to-be-true" news is so positive, why are they broadcasting it?

9 An illustration of testing strategies

The following is an illustration in testing three related strategies: Growth, Russell and Russell without S&P 500 stocks. A strategy usually includes a screen (finding stocks) the holding period (a year in this illustration for a long-term hold for value stocks) and an exit strategy (that is not described here). They both share a few common parameters such as EY (Earnings Yield). "Russell" only includes Russell 1000 stocks (the largest 1,000 stocks) and the other "Russell" excludes S&P 500 stocks (for potential candidates to be included in S&P 500).

For this testing I used a system that has historical data. The test starts on 1/1/2021 and ends on 6/1/2023 (today is 9/7/2023) with a new test every month. Each test starts on the first day of the month (or next trade day) and ends about a year away. The following table includes only 2 out of 29 tests and the summary results.

Start	RSP[1]	Growth	Russell	Russell
Date				wo S&P500
...				
09/1/21	-16%	-36%	No data	No Data
10/1/21	-14%	-18%	-10%	-19%
...				
Summary				
Average	-2%	16%	10%	7%
Beat RSP		807%	523%	404%
2021	-8%	2%	-11%	-17%
Beat RSP		122%	-40%	-122%
2022	-1%	19%	9%	6%
Beat RSP		3850%	1800%	1383%
2023	2%	28%	29%	37%
Beat RSP		1675%	1725%	2213%
Bear[2]	-11%	-8%	-1%	-9%
Beat RSP		24%	93%	12%
Bull[2]	3%	28%	20%	23%
Beat RSP		724%	471%	571%

[1] RSP represents the S&P 500 (the market for most) better than the weighted SPY.
[2] RSP have negative returns in most of these months from 7/1/21 to 4/1/22(as opposed to the Bull market from 7/1/22 to today).

Explanation

- These three strategies all beat the market (-2% in my tests): 16%, 10% and 7% in my tests.
- In the bear market (market timing could give some hints too) should give better results as most of the strategies selected few or even no stocks during these periods.
- I skipped tests when there is screened stock for all three strategies.
- The strategy without screened stocks I enter "null", which will not be included in averages.
- I screened producing a maximum of 20 stocks, then sorted them by a metric, and use the top five for tests. In actual trading, I further evaluate each screened stock as potential lawsuits, sector direction, politics... are not included in strategies.
- Sometimes you may want to exclude stocks that appear from several consecutive months as they would distort the performance results. For diversification, I do not buy stocks I already owned, but there are exceptions.
- 2021 is not a good year for Russell strategies and they both do not beat the market in this year.
- The strategies are long term. For short term such as strategies based on momentum, use 1, 2, or 3 months for durations.
- Your tests should reflect as closely on what you do in actual trading.
- The calculations can be easily done using a spreadsheet.
- I should also include the most favorable sectors for the periods.
- As in my convention in this book, all the returns do not include dividends, fees and commissions. Making the tests perfect could be too time consuming.
- This is a suggestion of what I test strategies. Personalize your own testing. Few successful investors would show you their secrets similar to here. To speed up testing, I used annualized returns and some end dates were within 6 months (not recommended if you have time for testing).

#Filler: Market Predictions: Handle with Caution
No economist, Fed chair, or Nobel laureate can forecast a crash accurately. Treat every prediction—even mine—as a hypothesis. Your own analysis and risk controls should guide your decisions.

#Filler: Defining a Market Plunge
A plunge runs from peak to trough—often over a year or two. While no indicator nails tops or bottoms perfectly, disciplined

chart-based signals help you avoid the worst and re-enter before the big rebound.

Section II: Safer strategies

Super-safe strategies

These strategies are designed for people who want *minimal effort* and *maximum safety*—the classic "orphans and widows" approach. The idea is that you have better things to do than worry about the stock market, and you may not want (or have time) to learn about investing in detail.

However, keep in mind: **most of these strategies won't beat inflation in the long run—except for the last one described here.**

Strategy #1: Certificates of Deposit (CDs) and Long-Term Treasury Bills

These are among the lowest-risk investments available. They require almost no effort aside from renewing maturing CDs. Still, there are important points to consider:

- **Mind the insurance limits.**
  Don't exceed government deposit insurance. As of 2019, the FDIC insures up to $250,000 per depositor, per insured bank, per ownership category.
- **Expect low returns.**
  CDs often fail to keep up with inflation. In our capitalist system, you're effectively penalized for not taking any risk or making any effort to invest.
- **Be cautious with complex offerings.**
  Mortgage-backed bonds or products dressed up as "safe" CDs can lose value completely, as many investors learned with Lehman Brothers' collapse.
- **Avoid callable CDs.**
  Banks will call them back when it benefits them, not you.
- **Strategic timing for Treasury Bills.**
  - Buy *long-term* Treasury bills when rates are high (e.g., 5% or more).
  - Buy *short-term* bills when rates are low (e.g., under 2%).
    Even though you'll get your principal plus interest at maturity, the market value of these bonds fluctuates inversely with interest rates.

- **Consider mutual funds or ETFs.**
  Most investors access Treasury bills through funds or ETFs for convenience.

Strategy #2: Annuities

For retirees, annuities can offer guaranteed lifetime income. But you need to understand that annuity terms are set by the companies selling them—to their advantage.

If you think they're in business to give you a comfortable retirement at their own expense, think again. Few annuity providers have low fees. Ask the salesperson how much commission they'll earn; you may want to run for the exit.

From my own experience:
I bought an annuity while working to defer taxes on investment gains. Over decades it did well (partly by rotating among sectors offered in the annuity—plus some luck). But I now expect higher taxes after age 70½, when mandatory retirement-account withdrawals kick in. Overall, the trading and management fees were not cheap compared to ETFs.

Still, annuities can be useful:
- They're good if you'd rather focus on other things in life than watch the market.
- They may reduce taxes if your tax bracket drops in retirement (as it often does).
- In a market plunge, annuities and CDs/Treasuries can outperform riskier investments.

As of April 2024, for example, my Fidelity annuities are positioned in Consumer Staples, Energy, Value Strategies, and Materials—reflecting caution in volatile markets.

Strategy #3: Rotating Between an ETF and Cash

This is a simple market-timing approach:
- Invest in SPY (or any ETF that tracks the overall market) when the outlook is good.
- Move into cash or a short-term Treasury-bond ETF when the market looks risky.

Though this book describes market timing in detail, the basic idea is straightforward: even beginners can manage it with just a few minutes of work each month.

This approach can outperform most mutual fund managers—who often aren't allowed to use market timing.

Getting started:
- Begin with a small allocation or test it on paper.
- Be aware there's some risk of false signals. But over the long term, "nothing risked, nothing gained" holds true.

#Filler: Black Swan
No EU country wants the war in Ukraine for its own benefit. No politician, not even a comedian-turned-president, wants to face an enemy with tanks at the gate. War can turn a wealthy nation into the poorest in its region.

Filler: A Personal Aside: "I Don't Have a Life"

I don't smoke.
I rarely drink.
I don't gamble.
I don't chase wild women (though the reverse is debatable).

Once, a restaurant hostess asked me:

"So… what do you do for fun?"

After a long pause, I replied:

"Nothing."

That's when I realized: I may not have vices—but maybe I don't really have a life either.

10 · Tom's conservative strategy

Below is a summary of Tom's conservative investing approach, adapted from his profile on Seeking Alpha. Treat it as an example you can modify to fit your own philosophy.

Key mindset: Ignore friends bragging about how much they're making in a rising market. And don't tell them how much you're *not* losing—unless you want fewer friends!

Link for Kindle readers: Tom's Strategy: (http://tonyp4idea.blogspot.com/2012/05/tom-armisteads-investment-strategy.html)

Note on timing: Ignore the original posting date—this strategy is designed to be evergreen. While it underperformed from 2009 to 2015 due to an unusually long bull market, it should comfortably outperform ultra-safe strategies like CDs and annuities over the long run.

A "Couch Potato" Strategy

My friend John uses a similar approach with great results and minimal risk. His method:

- **Buy stocks only after major market crashes.**
- **Sell when the market recovers.**

He ignores market pundits and focuses on big-picture timing—a great approach for those with no time or desire to monitor the market daily.

For example:

- He bought heavily in 2008–2010 and sold after 2010 for strong gains.
- He missed the big rally from 2010 to 2018. But such long uninterrupted bull markets are rare.

Even so, I'd bet he's still outperformed many mutual fund managers—despite spending almost no time on his investments.

Enhancing a Good Strategy

You can improve on Tom's and John's approach by following market-cycle stages discussed in this book:

- **Early Recovery Phase:** Buy SPY (or a market ETF) about 1½ years after a crash, or use the entry signals described in the Market Timing chapter.
- **Exit:** Sell SPY one or two years later.

Other Timing Options (If You Have Time)
- **Seasonal strategy:** Buy stocks or a market ETF on November 1, sell on May 1. Personally, I prefer buying on October 15 and selling on April 15 to beat the herd.
- **Best two months:** Buy December 1, sell February 1. Historically, this is the best period of the year.
- **Election cycle:** Buy in the year before an election, sell after a year.
- **Bond rotation:** Buy long-term bonds when interest rates exceed 5%; switch to short-term bonds or cash when rates drop below 2%.
- **Market timing:** Use my simple timing techniques from this book to exit and reenter the market with better risk management.

Bottom line: Spend the rest of your time relaxing on your couch— or enjoying a tropical drink on a sunny island! Just remember, markets aren't always rational, and all investing carries some risk.

An Alternative to Tom's Strategy
Here's a variation for active investors who want a rule-based approach:
- Maintain a watchlist of value stocks, updating it every 3 months.
- When the overall market drops 5%, set buy targets at 2% below current prices, or 5% below your watchlist prices.
- Set clear exit rules (e.g., sell at +12% gain or -12% loss).
- Consider holding longer if market conditions are calm.
- This approach works best in sideways markets—not during steep market plunges.

John's Approach
John stays about 75% in cash, buying only blue-chip stocks hitting 52-week lows. He doesn't care if friends are making money in a bull market.

My suggested tweaks (for those willing to accept more risk):

- Maintain 50% cash instead of 75%, and 0% cash in the Early Recovery phase.
- Expand your universe to all stocks with market caps over $1 billion, focusing on those within 5% of their recent lows.
- Always evaluate the fundamentals before buying—some stocks hitting new lows may be headed to zero.

Jill's Strategy

Jill doesn't have time to manage her portfolio actively, so she subscribes to an investment research service. Her process:

- Create a list of target stocks.
  - For example, choose stocks with a Value Line Safety rank of 1 or 2, or a VST score above 1.25 in VectorVest.
- When a stock hits her target price, she does a second round of research.
  - She checks her subscription service's analysis and the fundamental ratings at Fidelity.com.
- If the fundamentals look strong, she buys—and typically holds until market risk rises.

#Filler: Miss Mia

Back in my first job, not long after the Vietnam War, everyone in the office—men and women alike—tried to win over my stunning officemate, Mia. Everyone except me.

I figured if we ever got married, her name would become Mia Pow. You know... *MIA* as in "Missing In Action," and *POW* as in "Prisoner of War." Talk about making headlines without ever showing her face.

Of course, if she ever became a mom, we all know what she'd be called: *Mamma Mia.*

11 Defining swing trading

Swing trading is broadly defined as **anything that is not "buy and hold."** Unlike traditional buy-and-hold investors, swing traders actively manage their positions based on market conditions.

While buy-and-hold works well for some companies in their first decade of growth, it often disappoints in later years. Even index ETFs, which regularly rebalance to include stronger stocks, can be vulnerable to market bubbles.

In my view, the old "buy and hold" approach has been effectively dead since 2000. Major crashes have produced average declines of 45%, and there's been far less enthusiasm for buy-and-hold strategies in the investing press since then.

Instead, swing trading is about *"buy but not forget."* You exit when the market turns risky and reenter later—using the market timing methods described in this book.

Before choosing any style, evaluate:
- Your goals
- Your available time
- Your portfolio size

Types of Swing Trading

I break swing trading into **long-term** (6–12 months) and **short-term** (1–6 months) categories. This book covers both.

Though many tools overlap, **long-term swing** trading relies more on **fundamentals** (like P/E ratios), while **shorter-term** swing trading uses **momentum** metrics (like moving averages).

For reference, here are even shorter-term trading styles:
- **Momentum:** under 1 month
- **Rotation:** 1–2 months
- **Insider trading-based:** ~3 months
- **Headline-driven:** 1–3 months
- **Day trading:** 1 day (not covered here)

Note: Holding periods are guidelines only.

First rule: **never buy if the overall market is risky.** For long-term swings, focus on value stocks.

1. Long-Term Swing Trading (6–12 months)

This is my own most profitable approach—simple, effective, and lower effort.

- **Buy** stocks with strong fundamental metrics.
  Value investing is "swimming against the tide," so expect it to take 6+ months for the market to recognize the value.
- **Review** after 6 months.
  - If fundamentals remain strong, continue holding.
  - If they worsen, sell.
    Ideally, aim to hold for over a year to qualify for long-term capital gains rates (check current tax laws).
- **Be flexible.**
  Major events (lawsuits, new competitors, product failures) require reevaluation.
- **Stay informed.**
  - Use Seeking Alpha's portfolio tracker for news and articles.
  - Check Finviz.com for updates.

Most wealthy investors use a version of this method:
- Buffett holds for years or decades.
- Soros and Rogers look at long-term economic trends.

2. Short-Term Swing Trading (1–3 months)

This is what most people think of when they hear "swing trading"—and it's far harder than long-term swing trading.

Contrary to popular belief, it's the **hardest** way to make money. Most beginners lose to experienced, disciplined traders.

This book includes many chapters on technical analysis to help you get started.

Important: Books can't replace real experience with real money.
My recommendations:
- Master one or two indicators (e.g., Simple Moving Averages, or SMA). Don't use too many you don't understand.
- Screen stocks on Finviz.com using technical criteria.

- Take courses from experienced traders if you want to speed up learning.

Example strategy with SMA:

- Buy when price crosses above the moving average.
- Sell when it crosses below.

It's simple but effective—especially with high-volume, large-cap stocks.

- Common timeframes: SMA-20 for ~1-month trades, SMA-50 and SMA-200 for longer.
- On Finviz.com charts, you'll see these plotted automatically.

Pro tips:

- Backtest different SMA values on the stock's history.
- Expect to spend more time on short-term trades. Don't manage more than ~15 stocks at once.
- Technical analysis can be even better for timing **market or sector** moves than individual stocks.

Other useful indicators:

- Bollinger Bands
- MACD
- RSI(14)
- Patterns like Double Bottoms, Golden Crosses, Inverted Head & Shoulders

Tip: Start with one or two and really learn them before risking real money.

3. Momentum Trading

A variation of short-term swing trading with an ~1-month horizon.

- Buy momentum stocks; sell within a month.
- Use subscription services with "timeliness" scores for picks.
  - For example, I used these with good results (though I stopped when the market turned risky).
  - My annualized return was around 100% in 2013 and 50% in early 2014 (inflated by ignoring idle cash).

Alternative:

- Use free tools like Finviz.com's momentum screen.
- Look for strong technical trends yourself.

4. Trading on Headlines

- News often drives short-term market moves.

- Evaluate news fast and trade quickly.
- I've had some success with ETFs and individual stocks this way, though I haven't done enough to draw broad conclusions.

5. Sector Momentum / Rotation
- Finding the exact bottom is hard; tracking trends is easier.
- I rotate among sector ETFs or annuity subaccounts monthly, buying last month's winners (when market conditions are safe).

6. Following Insider Buying
- Insider purchases (especially by CEOs or CFOs) can signal value.
- Always check fundamentals, and beware of traps.
- Look for increasing volume following insider buying.
- Use resources like OpenInsider.com.
- I check insider purchases monthly.

Summary Table for Swing Strategies

Strategy	Avg. Duration (months)	Fundamental Weight (%)	Technical Weight (%)
Long-Term	6–12	100	0
Short-Term	3	50	50
Momentum	1	20	80
Headlines	varies	10	90
Sector Rot.	1–2	10	90
Insider	1–3	50	50

Explanation:
- For long-term swing, reevaluate every 6 months.
- Headline and insider strategies need fast reactions.
- Fundamentals matter more for longer-term holding.
- For short-term trades, favor momentum and technical analysis.

My Additions to Improve Results
- **Market Timing:**
  Sell most holdings during market plunges. While it's hard to sell at the exact peak, avoiding large drawdowns (like in 2000 and 2008) is key. Expect some false signals.
- **Diversify Properly:**

- o   Under $1M portfolio: ≤15 stocks, ≤3 in one sector.
- o   Over $1M: ~20 stocks.
    Too many stocks can dilute focus. Too few can increase risk.
- **Stock Criteria:**
    - o   Price > $2
    - o   Avg. daily volume > 10,000 shares (or 8,000 if price > $20)
    - o   Market cap > $200 million
    - o   Listed on major exchanges
        Most big winners tend to be in the $2–$12 range with market caps of $200M–$800M—often ignored by big institutions.
- **Be Skeptical of Subscription Services:**
    - o   Many boast unrealistic, cherry-picked returns.
    - o   Survivorship bias (ignoring bankrupt stocks) distorts backtests.
    - o   If their strategy was truly making 5,000%, why sell it?

Slow, consistent profits usually beat flashy, risky bets.

12   Top-down investing

Top-down investing is straightforward, but powerful:

- Only buy stocks when the overall market is favorable.

- Then choose the best-performing sector or industry.

- Finally, pick the strongest stock(s) within that sector.

This layered approach dramatically improves your chances of success. It's simple, proven, and practiced by many seasoned investors, myself included—even though it's surprisingly underused.

Here's a practical plan you can adapt:

Step 1: Avoid Bad Markets

Rule #1: Don't invest when the overall market is plunging.

This book describes simple, reliable ways to spot major downturns—no paid tools or subscriptions needed. Avoiding crashes is half the battle.

Step 2: Pick the Right Sector or Industry

Next, choose the best sector or industry. Most sectors have their own ETFs for easy research and investing.

For example:

- *Technology* (sector)

- *Computer Hardware* and *Software* (subsectors or industries)

For simplicity, I often just say "sector," as many free sites don't subdivide further.

To find strong candidates:

- Look at last month's best-performing sectors on sites like Seeking Alpha or financial news outlets.

- ETFs make it easy to track or invest directly.

Tip for Value Investors:
Instead of chasing the hottest sector, look for undervalued ones. This approach requires patience—holding for 6 months or more so the market recognizes true value.

Understanding Sector Rotation

Institutional investors (who control ~75% of trading volume) rotate money between sectors as profit potential changes.

Tracking this "smart money" rotation is essential. Use stop-loss orders to limit downside if the sector falls out of favor.

If you don't want to research individual stocks:

- Consider just trading sector ETFs.

- This lets you skip the next step entirely.

Step 3: Select the Best Stocks in the Sector

Once you've picked a strong sector, identify the best stocks within it.

Evaluate them using:

- **Fundamental analysis** (financial health, valuation)

- **Intangible factors** (brand, management)

- **Insider buying trends**

- **Institutional ownership patterns**

- **Technical analysis** (charts, price trends)

Don't be intimidated by these terms. In this book, I show simple, no-cost ways to analyze stocks without fancy subscriptions.

Step 4: Know When to Sell

Finally, always have a plan to reevaluate and exit positions:

- Sell if your fundamental thesis changes.

- Sell when your price target is met.

- Sell if broader market conditions turn risky.

Key principle: Repeat this disciplined process over and over.

A Simple Retirement Investing Plan

For long-term retirement planning:

- Live within your means and budget carefully.

- Buy durable, quality items that last.

- Save enough cash for emergencies and big planned expenses (vacations, cars, college, etc.).

- Invest leftover savings in a retirement account (Roth IRA if eligible), with a simple mix:

  - **80%** in a broad market ETF

  - **20%** in a short-term bond ETF

Once a month, check the market cycle chart described in this book:

- If it signals danger, move to cash.

- Reenter when conditions improve.

This approach beats many complex, high-fee financial plans.

Real-World Results (From My 2022 Book)

Here are *actual* recommendations I published:

Symbol (11)	Return	Annualized
ADES	-54%	-56%
AOSL	-34%	-35%
BLDR	-18%	-19%
BZH	-37%	-39%
DVN	73%	76%
MLI	19%	20%
MTDR	81%	84%

NUE	40%	41%
SCHN	-30%	-31%
UFPI	-5%	-5%
USAK	See below	
Average	4%	4%
RSP	-6%	-7%
Beat RSP by	153%	

USAK has not been shown in my historical database that has a survival bias. The recommended price as of 12/15/21 was $17.74 and the last price (09/14/2022) was $31.71 gaining 79% and annualized to 105%.

Lesson: Focusing on strong sectors would have improved results further:

- Energy (DVN +76%, MTDR +84%)

- Trucking (USAK +79%)

Afterthought

A late friend of mine followed a classic **buy-and-hold** strategy with big, reliable companies. It served him well:

- He died with millions in stocks plus a million-dollar house.

- His only error? Failing to gift more of his holdings before death, leading to higher estate taxes.

- The IRS turned out to be the biggest beneficiary.

Additional Notes

Understanding "Max Drawdown"
This is the worst-case loss you might face.
Example:

- Buy MSFT at $100.

- It drops to $50.

- Max drawdown = 50%.

If you're on margin, your broker will call you on the way down.

While long-term investors might wait for it to recover to $200, short-term traders must set tight stop-loss rules to control risk.

Section III: Riskier strategies

"Nothing risked, nothing gained."

From my book "Best Stocks to Buy for July, 2021", Sub List of risky stocks:

Commodity (3)	Return	Ann.
EVC	16%	43%
NUE	10%	26%
YELL	108%	283%
Average	45%	117%
RSP	1%	2%
Beat RSP by	5,275%	

The details can be found in the following link.
http://tonyp4idea.blogspot.com/2022/12/best-stocks-series.html

13   The Contrarian Approach

Contrarian investors deliberately go against prevailing market sentiment. They look for opportunities where crowd behavior has pushed prices to extremes—**buying when others are selling, and selling when others are buying.**

Timing is crucial. The goal isn't to oppose every move the market makes, but to recognize when sentiment has driven valuations too far. Typically, you'll ride the trend until assets become clearly **overvalued**, then reverse course.

When a stock or sector is **overbought**, a correction often follows. But there are exceptions. For example, gold can behave differently, with price trends shaped by factors like a weakening U.S. dollar and inflation-adjusted long-term demand.

⚠ *Important: Adopting a contrarian stance blindly is dangerous. The key is to analyze carefully whether the consensus view is actually wrong.*

When to Be Contrarian

Ask yourself: is current sentiment justified, or has the market overreacted? For instance:

- **Should you have invested in stocks after they fell sharply by July 2012?**
    - If the economy faced a **W-shaped recession**, waiting would have been smarter.
    - If conditions mirrored **Japan's "lost decades,"** patience was essential.
    - But if a **new secular bull market** was starting, waiting too long would mean missing big gains.

Similarly, massive money printing can drive inflation and lift asset prices despite weak fundamentals—a critical factor for contrarians to consider.

Sector-Specific Caution

Should you have bought:

- **Bank stocks immediately after 2008?**
- **Tech stocks right after the 2001 crash?**

With hindsight, the answer is often no. Many such stocks lost half their value but continued to decline or even went bankrupt because their core problems weren't resolved.

General Contrarian Guideline

- **Avoid investing broadly in equities for at least one year after a major market crash.**
- **Avoid the bubble-causing sectors for at least two years.**

This rule of thumb has held true in both the **2000** and **2007** bottoms. It isn't infallible—but it's a reliable starting point for disciplined contrarians.

Final Thought
Contrarian investing requires **patience, discipline, and rigorous analysis**. It's not about reflexively opposing the crowd—it's about identifying when the crowd is **wrong**.

Additional Tips
- If you have substantial assets but **no financial adviser** or **no professional research service**, you're at risk of making costly mistakes.
- Even elite teams can fail. **Long-Term Capital Management (LTCM)** had Nobel laureates, advanced models, and deep resources—but still collapsed spectacularly.
- Beware of **modern portfolio theory** if it relies on assumptions or testing that don't hold up in real markets.

Links
Contrarian
(http://en.wikipedia.org/wiki/Contrarian_investing

#Filler: I wish I have a time machine
After collecting bottles for money, an old lady ordered a bowl of plain rice and ate by herself. I wish I could have ordered a meat dish for her and I was 'ashamed' of being generous.

A well-dressed gentleman offered his just-bought hamburger to a beggar. The beggar refused and asked for money instead – most likely he needed the money to buy liquor. A tale of two citizens.

During a lunch with my fellow tourists, a beautiful girl danced for our entertainment. I did not offer her anything and it had been bothering me for years.

During college, my housemates asked me to apply for food stamps. I had used only a few stamps then as I did not cook. I feel ashamed as this is my only time to collect social welfare.
We have regrets in life and we can only bring them to our graves.

Overview of Contrarian Investing (written by ChatGPT)

Contrarian investing is a strategy that involves going against prevailing market trends or sentiment. Instead of following the crowd, contrarian investors seek opportunities where others see risk, pessimism, or underperformance. The core belief is that markets often overreact—both on the upside and downside—and these overreactions can create profitable opportunities.

Core Principles
Buy When Others Sell
Contrarians look to buy assets that are undervalued due to excessive fear or neglect. This often means purchasing stocks or sectors during market downturns or crises.

Sell When Others Buy
On the flip side, contrarian investors may exit or avoid assets that are overhyped or overpriced due to excessive optimism or speculative bubbles.

Market Psychology Matters
The crowd is often wrong at turning points. Contrarians pay close attention to investor sentiment, media coverage, and market extremes.

Key Indicators for Contrarian Opportunities
Sentiment Surveys: High bullish sentiment may indicate a market top; extreme pessimism may signal a bottom.

Valuation Metrics: Look for low P/E, P/B, or P/FCF ratios in out-of-favor stocks or sectors.

Insider Buying: Executives buying company stock during downturns may signal confidence.

Short Interest: High short interest could suggest the stock is oversold and due for a reversal.

Historical Cycles: Markets and sectors tend to move in cycles; contrarians often buy at the troughs.

Famous Contrarian Investors
Warren Buffett: Known for "being greedy when others are fearful and fearful when others are greedy."
Sir John Templeton: Made fortunes by investing in deeply depressed markets, such as post-WWII Japan.
David Dreman: Advocated for buying low P/E and low price-to-book stocks when others shunned them.

Benefits of Contrarian Investing
Potential for Outsized Returns: Buying undervalued assets can lead to significant gains if markets correct.

Psychological Edge: Contrarians aren't swayed by hype or fear, helping them avoid common investor pitfalls.

Diversification of Strategy: It adds a layer of strategic differentiation from momentum or growth investing.

Risks and Challenges
Timing: Markets can remain irrational longer than expected. Being early can feel the same as being wrong.

Value Traps: Some assets are cheap for a reason. Not all contrarian plays bounce back.

Emotional Discipline: Going against the crowd requires conviction and the ability to withstand criticism and short-term losses.

Examples of Contrarian Opportunities
2008 Financial Crisis: Buying bank stocks when they were heavily punished.

Tech Crash (2000–2002): Entering non-tech sectors as tech collapsed.

Pandemic Sell-off (March 2020): Buying quality stocks at deep discounts when panic selling hit the markets.

Conclusion
Contrarian investing is not about blindly opposing the majority—it's about making informed decisions when the market overreacts. The most successful contrarians combine deep research, valuation analysis, and psychological resilience. In the long run, those who can think independently and act decisively in times of uncertainty often reap the greatest rewards.

Filler: Insider trading

First, the stocks are bought or sold by insiders and their relatives, then followed by programmed computers, institutional investors, technicians and then retail investors.

14 Refined "Dogs of the Dow" strategy

Overview
The "Dogs of the Dow" is a well-known, simple dividend-based strategy used even by some professional fund managers. The idea is straightforward:
- At year-end, buy the 10 Dow Jones Industrial Average (DJIA) stocks with the highest dividend yields.
- Hold them for a year, then repeat the process annually.
- Be sure to exclude stocks whose dividends mainly reflect return of capital.

For more on the classic strategy:
Wikipedia: Dogs of the Dow:
http://en.wikipedia.org/wiki/The_Dogs_of_the_Dow

Historical Performance
As of 2014, the traditional Dogs strategy outperformed the Dow and S&P 500 by only a modest margin over the prior decade. However, it performed quite well in the four years leading up to 2014, partly due to a mild bubble in dividend-growth stocks.

Caution: Stay alert for any dividend-stock "bubble" that might eventually burst.

From Wikipedia:
"In fact, the Dogs of the Dow and Small Dogs of the Dow struggled to keep up with the Dow during latter stages of the dot-com boom (1998 and 1999) as well as during the financial crisis (2007–2009)."

My Suggestions to Improve Results
Here are ways to strengthen the strategy and reduce risk:
1. **Avoid extremely high expected P/Es** (> 35) or companies with P/E ≤ 0 (for example, many dot-com stocks in 2000).
2. **Exclude vulnerable sectors** during specific risks:
   o Banks in 2007.
   o Travel-related companies during the 2020 pandemic.
3. **Use market timing:**
   o Avoid buying during major market plunges.
   o Reenter equities in the "Early Recovery" phase of the market cycle (defined in this book).

Customizing for Better Performance

When a strategy becomes widely used, it often underperforms—because everyone is doing the same thing.

One easy variation:

- Instead of buying the 10 highest-yield Dow stocks, first **sort them by forward (expected) P/E in ascending order**.
- Buy the **top 5 with positive earnings**, skipping those with zero or negative earnings.

Result (backtested for illustration only):

- Average annualized return of ~15% (12% price appreciation + ~3% dividends) from November 1, 2000 to November 1, 2010.

Another variant:

- Buy the top 5 candidates on **November 1** and sell on **May 1** the next year to benefit from the statistically strong November–April period.

Additional Refinements to Consider

You can further improve or adapt the strategy with these variations:

1. **Expand the universe:**
   - Include S&P 500 and NASDAQ stocks, not just the Dow.
2. **Adjust timing:**
   - Execute between **Dec. 1 and Dec. 15** instead of early January to avoid the herd effect.
3. **Use favorable seasonal windows:**
   - Buy on **Nov. 1** and sell on **May 1**—works well for retirement accounts or to offset short-term losses.
4. **Filter on valuation:**
   - Sort top 10 dividend payers with positive earnings by ascending P/E.
   - Buy the top 5, avoiding those with P/E < 4 (can signal problems) or extremely high debt/equity ratios (unless typical for the sector).
5. **Sector exclusions:**
   - Avoid lenders, drug companies, miners, insurers, and emerging-market stocks.
6. **Legal risk filter:**
   - Skip companies facing serious lawsuits. Minor ones are acceptable.

7. **Short interest filter:**
   o Avoid stocks with 10–20% short interest (shares shorted / float).
   o However, >30% short interest might suggest potential for a short squeeze—could be opportunistic.
8. **Market cycle timing:**
   o Don't use the strategy in the first year after a major market plunge.

Why This Works
These refinements help avoid crowded trades, bubbles, and risky outliers—making it a **lazy person's** method for stock picking and market timing that still outperforms the basic "Dogs" strategy.

Afterthoughts on Testing and Implementation
When testing your customized strategy:
- Use recent data (ideally the last 10+ years) to ensure it still works.
- Adjust valuation filters if you're risk-averse (e.g., only buy P/E between 4 and 12).
- Experiment with different **holding periods** (6 months, 11 months, 12 months).
- Consider **contra-ETFs** (inverse funds) during unfavorable stock periods (May 1 to Nov. 1), though avoid them in secular bull markets.
- Automate backtests as much as possible to test different combinations.
- Be wary of "data fitting" just to get pretty backtest results.
- Test your approach for **all market cycle stages**.
- Always **annualize returns** for easier comparison.
- Expect real-life performance to lag backtest results.

Pro tip:
If you find one approach that tests at 60% annualized and another at 20% under the same conditions, favor the better one—but verify carefully.

Implementation Advice
- **Paper trade first** to gain confidence.
- Start small when committing real money.
- Remember: There is no "Holy Grail." Markets change and are not always rational.

- Still—investing with a well-researched, disciplined strategy is far better than going in blind.

Link: https://www.youtube.com/watch?v=Jwf8wrtDKGo
Link: 1 https://www.youtube.com/watch?v=9icBf8iZXbc

15 Multi baggers

Finding the next Apple—an investment that multiplies your money many times over—is one of the most rewarding goals in investing. It's possible, but not easy. For every big winner you uncover, you'll likely sift through many losers.

How to Find Potential Multi-Baggers

I use a screen that focuses on **companies doubling sales and profits year over year** (comparing the same quarter to avoid seasonal effects).

Typically, these are:
- **Small-cap or penny stocks**, often under $10, and frequently not listed on major exchanges at first.
- **Non-dividend-paying**—they reinvest heavily in R&D.

Many good candidates show up at least **one year post-IPO**, when they have enough financial history. This timing also weeds out companies that fail early.

Key Characteristics
- Prices often hover between **$2–$10** before breaking out.
- Stocks under $5 are often **non-marginable**, limiting demand.
- Breakouts on **high volume** can signal big moves.

When a stock is taking off:
- RSI(14) often stays **above 65** for years.
- Always assess **reward/risk**. If the odds of doubling equal the odds of halving, consider selling half. Remember: no one ever went broke taking profits.

Examples:
- **SMCI** – my own 12-bagger (sold some before the top).
- **TTWO** – still performing well.

On IPOs

Types of IPOs:

- From companies with **established products** (e.g., Facebook) — typically less risky.
- From **new, unproven companies** — higher risk.

Historically:

- Roughly **40%** of IPOs make money in their first year.
- **60%** lose value early on.

IPOs raise crucial funds for R&D and marketing. Before buying, ask:

- Is the product **truly innovative**?
- Is it likely to become **profitable**?

IPO Investing Realities

- Many retail investors **can't access IPO shares** at the offer price without broker connections.
- Often the best gains are made by **buying early post-IPO** if the company shows real promise.
- Some legendary winners—**Microsoft, Walmart, Tesla**— rewarded early post-IPO investors richly.

However, be aware of the **common IPO lifecycle**:

1. Founders and early investors cash in.
2. Early investors profit.
3. Stock price surges; insiders eventually sell after lock-up.
4. Retail investors often hold too long and take the losses when the stock declines.

Lesson: You're buying the company's **future vision**. Review progress regularly. A "hot" product may fail due to competition or regulation.

Evaluating IPOs Beyond Year One

- Year 1 is often a **honeymoon phase** with less attention to fundamentals.
- In Year 2+, evaluate using **fundamental metrics**:
    - **P/E ratio**: If over 50, be cautious—price may have run too far.
    - **Debt/Equity**: High debt increases bankruptcy risk.

Example: Cisco was once a top-valued company, crashed, then recovered by 2013. Use **fundamental** and **technical analysis** (like SMA) to guide trades.

Managing Winners

- Be mindful of **insider lock-up expiration** post-IPO—selling pressure can hit prices.
- As prices rise, keep checking **valuation metrics**:
  - P/E under 35? Reasonable, but check **PEG** too.
- Use **stop-loss orders** to lock in profits.

Typically, after 10 years, even successful companies see **slower price growth**. Finding the peak is hard. A good compromise? **Sell half** if unsure.

Turnaround Plays

Not every fallen stock is doomed. Some bounce back. Clues:

- Insider buying.
- Staircase patterns: price stabilizes, then jumps.

Expect More Losers Than Winners

Most small companies fail. Survival bias hides them in databases. If your backtests don't account for this, results will look deceptively good.

Bottom line:

- Have **long-term, risk-tolerant capital**.
- Expect many failures.
- A few big winners can more than compensate.

Historical context:

- Apple, Microsoft, Oracle succeeded due to **generational products**.
- Recent IPOs like Zynga or Groupon suggest fewer obvious winners today.

No stock justifies a **forward P/E over 40** without exceptional potential (e.g., a breakthrough drug).

IPO Market Trends

- **2015** was a poor IPO year—average NYSE IPO dropped ~15% on its first day.
- Hong Kong led in IPO value, mostly Chinese firms.
- Shenzhen Exchange was highly volatile but supported emerging tech companies.

Tax Considerations

- Sell losers to offset gains.
- For big winners, consider:
  - Holding until death for **stepped-up basis** (no capital gains for heirs under 2016 rules).

- ○ Donating appreciated stock for tax deductions.
- Always consult a **tax advisor**.

My Experience
- I often **sell when stocks double**.
- Rarely hold long enough for a **triple-bagger** unless acquired or held for long-term gains.
- Best practice: **Use trailing stops** to protect gains as price rises.

Spotting the Next Big Wave
Multi-baggers come from companies that **change the world**. These often:

- Start with **venture capital**, then small exchanges, then major listings.
- By the time the mass market notices them, much of the upside is gone.

I've seen many in 30 years but missed acting early—often out of caution. Examples:

- **Apple, Microsoft, Google, Cisco** – tempted to sell too soon after early gains.
- **Pharma** – some success via newsletters and insider data.
- **Retail disruption** – Walmart's China strategy; Amazon's e-commerce revolution.

Strategies to Identify and Manage Them
- Use **technical analysis** (SMA) to time entries and exits.
- Adjust **stop-loss orders** as the stock appreciates.
- Watch for **new technologies or regulatory shifts** creating demand (e.g., legalization trends, new distribution channels).

Future Opportunities
Emerging markets, especially **China**, may see more innovative companies due to:

1. A large pool of well-trained scientists and engineers.
2. Government support for science and tech.
3. Lower labor costs and longer work hours.
4. A massive internal market.

But **beware of data quality issues** in developing markets.

IPO Trading Tips
- Most retail investors can't buy IPO allocations directly.

- Avoid buying in the first few volatile days.
- Consider buying after **new highs** confirm strength.
- Be cautious before insiders' lock-up expires (typically 6–12 months).

IPO Calendar: https://www.nasdaq.com/market-activity/ipos

16 Trading by headlines

Headline-driven trading means reacting quickly to major news events that can move markets. It can be **profitable**— but it's also risky, time-consuming, and requires quick decision-making and solid discipline.

Example: The 2019 G20 Trade Truce
On June 29, 2019, Trump and Xi signaled a trade truce at the G20. Markets were poised to rally the following Monday. I had just closed a short position and expected:

- Chip stocks to rise as trade restrictions on Huawei eased.
- Shipping companies to benefit from renewed trade flows.
- Agriculture to rebound, helping farmers and suppliers.

Without overcomplicating, I scanned shipping stocks and saw weekend gains over 4% in names like **DHT, NM, SBLK, STNG, TNK, and ASC**. Acting quickly is essential: markets digest news fast, and opportunities vanish if you're too slow.

Sector Rotation Insight
I exchanged ideas with sector rotation expert Andrew McElroy. He emphasizes:
"More potential for profit (and loss) exists in individual sectors, especially when the index is moving sideways. I buy strong sectors on pullbacks to support and avoid overbought sectors at resistance. Elliott Wave helps identify cycles of buying and selling."

News and Macroeconomic Headlines
Many headlines can be trading catalysts:

- Presidential elections and policy changes
- Interest rate hikes
- New regulations
- Trade agreements or wars
  For example:
- **Rain in Brazil?** Coffee futures typically rise.
- **Heavy rain in SE Asia?** Rice futures would respond (though no rice ETF exists).
- **Flooding or drought?** Corn prices surge.

Similarly, wars in the Middle East can boost oil prices. Buy oil ETFs on rising tensions and sell when the risk recedes. Small, consistent profits can add up.

Caution: Don't Trade Blindly

Headline trading is **not for everyone**:

- The media often **exaggerates** news for clicks and ad sales.
- Stock recommendations are usually **stale** or **manipulative**.
- Always **do your own research**.
  Many casual investors watch headlines all day but make no money. With planning and practice, they could become "couch-potato millionaires"—but only if they test and refine their approach carefully.

Rules for Trading Headlines

1. **Stay unemotional**. Learn from past wins and losses, but don't chase them.
2. **Don't bet the farm**. Use options, ETFs, or small positions.
3. **Act quickly**. Today's headline is old news tomorrow.
4. **Winners and losers are linked**. Apple's iPhone boom hurt BlackBerry.
5. **Ensure after-hours trading access** if needed.
6. **Plan your exit** for both gains and losses.
7. **Evaluate fast**. Avoid companies with poor fundamentals; consider sector ETFs instead.
8. **Assume others know first**. Look for insights you can anticipate ahead of time.
9. **Value investing works too**. I recommended oil at $30/barrel in January 2016. It was cheap, but required patience.
10. **Sometimes fundamentals can be ignored short-term** if the headline is powerful enough.

Quick 5-Minute Stock Check (Finviz.com)

- Look for more **green** than **red** in metrics.
- **Forward P/E** under 20, positive earnings.
- **Debt/Equity** under 50%.
- **P/FCF** not highlighted in red.
- **SMA20/SMA50** trends—upward momentum.
- Recent **insider buying** is a positive sign.
- Be cautious with **foreign** and **low-volume** stocks.
  If most of these pass quickly, consider it—but remember: **nothing is 100% certain**.

When Headline Trading Doesn't Work
- In severe market plunges, buying on bad news can backfire.
- Media hype can cause overreactions in either direction.
- Scheduled events (earnings, unemployment data, Fed meetings) are often priced in ahead of time.

Using Deduction
Anticipate impacts before the headline hits:
- A bumper grain harvest in China? U.S. farmers might struggle. Watch companies like Deere, Potash, Monsanto.
- Rising meat demand in China? Corn and fertilizer use rises—fertilizer companies benefit.

Geopolitical Crises
Sometimes the best move is **no move**. After 9/11, my stop-loss orders sold too many positions. The market recovered quickly—but I missed the bounce.
Research from Ned Davis (1900–2014) suggests:
- Trade affected sectors in the **first few days**.
- Reverse or exit positions roughly **2 months later**.
  Example: Oil and gold typically spike early in geopolitical crises.

My Experiences
- **Interest rate trends**: Invest in rate-sensitive sectors accordingly.
- **CROX (2016)**: Dropped 40% in a day; I bought, made 10% in a week—but sold too soon. It later doubled.
- **Boeing 737 MAX crashes**: Missed shorting Boeing and its suppliers.
- **Apple's new iPod**: Missed buying component suppliers.
- **Uranium stocks**: Should have bought after Japan's nuclear disaster; they surged when reactors reopened.
- **2014**: Profitable trades on BBY and a small win on TGT—both driven by headlines.

Volatile Markets and Headlines
In years like 2012 and 2015 (pre-election years), markets were **sideways but volatile**, whipsawed by headlines:
- Buy on 3–5% dips from the last peak.
- Sell on 3–5% rallies from the last trough.

Trend and Calendar Timing

- Year-end tax selling often pressures losers—good entry points in December.
- Sometimes investors sell winners expecting tax hikes, creating buying opportunities (e.g., Apple in late 2012).
- **Investors are emotional**: Take advantage of irrational selling or buying.

Scheduled Events

- Many market-moving events are known in advance: earnings, jobs data, Fed meetings.
- Educated guesses on their outcomes often leak early. Example: Debt ceiling showdowns repeatedly caused ~5% market drops. Sell before the event, buy after resolution.

Following Institutions

Institutions **drive the market**. Watch their sector rotations. When they see a sector as overvalued, they move out.

Final Caveats

- Always **know the crisis**. A short-term shock is tradable; a true global disaster (e.g., WWIII) is not.
- There's no sure thing in trading. The goal is to make **educated guesses** that pay off more often than not.

#Filler: Cooperation vs. Confrontation

Can music unite the world? I'd like to believe so—if only we, and the Chinese, could stop letting blind and dumb nationalism cloud our vision.

Take this example: a Chinese musician named Moyun plays Hotel California—one of America's greatest rock classics—on a traditional Chinese instrument. The result? Pure harmony. And it's being enjoyed by people all around the world.

Sometimes, a single song says more about cooperation than a thousand speeches.
Watch it here: https://www.youtube.com/watch?v=gf6v59c5yuY

17   Earnings season overreactions

Overview
Earnings season, which typically runs in January, April, July, and October, is known for sharp stock price moves.

AAII offers screens for positive and negative earnings surprises. Historically, the **"pleasant surprise"** screen has performed best. Zacks also ranks stocks based on positive earnings revisions. Their top-ranked (#1) stocks have reportedly delivered ~26% annual returns on average.

Caution: Always check recent performance (e.g., last 5 years). Strategies often lose their edge when too many investors pile in.

Timing Note:
Earnings announcements generally start in the first two weeks after the end of quarters (December, March, June, September).
Investopedia Explanation

My Approach
Contrary to popular advice, I often look for **negative surprises**.

If a company's problem seems temporary and there's a path to recovery, I'll buy after the drop. It might take months or even a year for the stock to rebound, but the "buy low, sell high" approach often works.

Example: A 1% earnings miss causing a 10% price drop can be a buying opportunity—*unless* it signals a real, long-term decline or looming bankruptcy.

On the other hand, my **momentum strategy** focuses on buying stocks with **positive earnings revisions**, usually holding for less than a month.

Macro Note:
Strong currency effects (like a strong USD) can hurt multinationals, as roughly 40% of their revenue comes from abroad (my estimate). In such times, consider **shorting** stocks likely to disappoint on earnings.

Key Lesson

Markets often **overreact**. Both retail and institutional investors are prone to emotional decisions.

- Fund managers may dump losers quickly to protect their jobs.
- Retail investors often sell late, following big institutional moves.

Learn to judge whether a selloff is an **overreaction** or the start of a **real decline**.

Hedging Earnings Risk

Earnings announcements can cause big, sudden price moves. You can manage risk with three main strategies:

1. **Stop-Loss Orders**
   - Automatically sell if the price drops below a set level.
   - Warning: Stocks can gap past stops.
   - Look for **unusually high volume** as a clue to institutional selling.
   - Make sure your broker allows **after-hours trades**.
2. **Options**
   - Buying puts or protective strategies works like insurance.
   - Not cheap—use for protecting against **big losses**, not routine volatility.
3. **Earnings Predictions**
   - Analysts publish "whispers" or refined forecasts.
   - Zacks offers a grading system for earnings quality.
   - Insiders know results early, but using non-public info is illegal.
   - Watch for **earnings revisions** ahead of announcements—often a strong signal.
   - Dividend announcements or increases can also boost stock prices.

Personal Note:

I rarely hedge this way because I own too many stocks. Instead, I focus on careful **stock selection** and **regular monitoring** to increase the odds of positive surprises.

Profiting from Earnings Surprises

Stock prices usually rise on positive surprises and fall on negative ones—but reactions can be extreme or irrational.

- Example: A 1% earnings miss can trigger a 10% drop.

- Occasionally, even a beat causes a drop if expectations were unrealistically high.

How to find opportunities:
- Screen for upcoming earnings announcements (e.g., Finviz.com, SeekingAlpha).
- Basic screening criteria:
  - Market Cap > $200M
  - Price > $2
  - Average daily volume > 10,000 shares
- If you subscribe to Zacks, focus on Grade 1 and Grade 2 stocks.
- Look for **meaningful insider buying**.
- Favor stocks with a **positive short-term trend** (e.g., 20-day SMA on Finviz).
- Also consider the **sector trend** (use sector ETFs as proxies).
- Read analysis on sites like SeekingAlpha for qualitative insights.

Tip: Don't expect 100% wins. Even with a **50% win rate**, you can do well. Avoid buying when the market as a whole is weak or earnings are widely expected to disappoint.

Exploiting Post-Earnings Moves
You can also try to **capture short-term price reactions** immediately after earnings announcements.
1. Make sure your broker allows **after-hours trading**.
2. Use Finviz to find stocks reporting earnings this week. Prefer fundamentally solid names.
   - Large-cap: Market Cap > $500M
   - Smaller-cap: Market Cap > $100M
3. Check EarningsWhispers.com for consensus and whisper estimates. Note the exact time of the release.
4. If you have Zacks, use its ratings as an extra filter.
5. Be ready **at least 15 minutes before** the scheduled announcement.
6. Use Google News to search the stock name and EPS. Refresh often for real-time updates.
7. If the company beats estimates:
   - Buy at least a penny below the last trade price.
   - Sell within a day or two to capture the post-announcement move.
   - Note: This doesn't always work.

8. Consider **including revenue surprises** in your assessment, not just EPS.

Personal Note:
I don't do this often—it's too time-consuming, and I prefer my sleep! But it can work if you're diligent.

Final Advice:
Always **test your approach before using real money**. There are many variables to adjust to your style and market conditions.

Bottom Line: Earnings season is full of opportunity—but also risk. With careful screening, smart timing, and good risk management, you can tilt the odds in your favor.

Filler
My friend's late uncle had a 'buy and hold strategy' that worked pretty well. Most of his stocks were big companies. He died with a house worth more than a million and many millions in stocks. His only mistake was not to transfer more of his stocks to his heirs before his death. He died in the year when the estate exemption was reduced to a million. Uncle Sam was the biggest winner and won big without any effort.

#Filler: A Common Investing Mistake
A frequent investing mistake is buying or avoiding a stock simply because you like—or dislike—its products. Your taste isn't the same as the market's. Investment decisions should be based on *growth potential*, not personal preference.

That said, steer clear of sin stocks if they conflict with your values. And while airlines may nickel-and-dime passengers at every turn, ironically, that penny-pinching could be a positive sign for investors.

#Filler: The Real Inflation Meter
You know inflation is out of control when a beggar turns down your spare change and asks for a full dollar.

Forget government stats—*this* is the inflation indicator that rarely hits home run.

And when the same beggar asks me to pay via Alipay... I realize China might be more advanced than we are.

18   Strategies on earnings

Here are two strategies on earnings. It is supposed to make millions for my children but they are not interested in investing. You either hate or love what your father does.

1. Buy the stocks with earnings announcement soon with Zacks rating 1 (the best) and short those with Zacks rating 5 (the worst). BY THE WAY, Zacks rating is free so far for individual stocks.

2. After the earnings announcement, Google the company every second or so. If the earnings are good, buy it fast with market order. If it is bad, short it.

Do not be greedy and set a limit on loss. Do not call me whether the trade is good or bad. In addition, check insider transactions and SMA-20.

I have tried #1 once a long while ago. I have not tried #2 as I have a life too. In the long run, these strategies should make you some money.

#Filler: iGeneration
These days, nearly everyone has an iPhone. Those of us in the lower economic tier—myself included—often carry knockoffs or "outdated" models that are, heaven forbid, several months old.

My granddaughter, barely a year old, already loves playing with the iPad. It keeps her entertained for hours. Before she could even say "Mom," her first word was "I"—as in iPad. At family gatherings, my cousins often sit side by side texting each other instead of talking. When they're not texting, they're playing games... still on their phones.

Somehow, with just one pair of eyes and one pair of ears, they manage to juggle an iPad, listen to an iPod, and text on an iPhone—all at once. Thank you, Apple, for redefining multitasking. Personally, I'd rather do one thing well than several things poorly.

Meanwhile, students in China and India are gaining ground, spending more time studying while many of our kids spend hours gaming. Do we really believe that trading study time for screen time won't have consequences down the road?

And perhaps the most awkward moment for some parents? Trying to explain to their kids that they exist only because a hurricane once knocked out the Wi-Fi—and with it, their iPads and iPhones. LOL. Digital tools are great, but moderation is key.

.

19   Strategies that worked before

Here are three once-popular strategies that performed well in the past but have struggled more recently. I've explored whether they can be revived or improved.

1. O'Shaughnessy's Strategy
Wikipedia link:
(http://en.wikipedia.org/wiki/James_O%27Shaughnessy)

This approach delivered excellent returns from 1954 to 1994. The original rules were:
- Buy 50 Dow stocks with:
  - The highest one-year returns,
  - Five consecutive years of rising earnings,
  - Price < 1.5 × corporate sales.

After he published it in a book, the edge faded—too many investors began using it. It's a classic case of a strategy losing effectiveness once it's widely known.

2. The Foolish Four
Wikipedia link: http://en.wikipedia.org/wiki/Foolish_Four
From Wikipedia:
"The Foolish Four is a discredited mechanical investing technique that, like the Dogs of the Dow, attempts to select Dow stocks that will outperform the average in the near future."
How it worked:
- For each Dow stock, divide its dividend yield by the square root of its price.
- Rank stocks by this number.
- Buy the 2nd, 3rd, 4th, and 5th highest-ranked stocks in equal dollar amounts. The top-ranked stock is excluded.

Though clever, the approach proved unreliable over time.

3. Buying the Highest ROE Stocks

This idea was popularized in investing books but often disappoints in practice. ROE is only one fundamental metric among many. Blindly chasing high ROE can backfire, and I don't see a good way to revive this strategy. Investors should replace it with better, multi-factor approaches.

My Take

All three of these strategies worked for a while. But once they were publicized and widely adopted, their effectiveness declined.

- The **ROE strategy** fails because it's too simplistic.
- **The Foolish Four** is too close to the Dogs of the Dow to add much new value.
- **O'Shaughnessy's approach**, however, has potential with thoughtful updates.

How to Revive O'Shaughnessy's Strategy

It's basically a long-term momentum strategy with a valuation filter. It could work again—especially if fewer people use it. Many screeners (like AAII) let you test similar approaches. Here's how I would modernize it:

What to Include

- Expand the universe:
  - S&P 500 stocks instead of only Dow 30.
  - Or all stocks on major US exchanges.
- Filter out penny stocks:
  - Price > $2 (or $5 for more conservative investors).
  - Average daily volume > 10,000 shares.
- Use **expected earnings** (forward-looking) instead of trailing twelve months.
- Exclude most emerging-market stocks for now.
- Apply a **fundamental scoring system** (like mine, described in my books) to screen candidates further.
- Perform full qualitative analysis of finalists.

Timing Suggestions

- **For retirement accounts:**
  - Buy around Nov. 1 and sell around May 1.
  - Or buy from mid-October to mid-April to get a slight edge and avoid the herd.

- **For taxable accounts:**
  - Buy in Nov/Dec.
  - Sell losers (held <1 year) for tax losses.
  - Hold winners >1 year to get better long-term capital gains treatment. *(Check your current Federal and state tax laws.)*
- **Risk control:**
  - Close out all positions if the market is plunging.
  - Consider selling covered calls on holdings with favorable long-term tax treatment.

Choosing How Many Stocks

- If too few candidates meet the criteria, consider relaxing requirements (e.g., 3 consecutive years of rising earnings instead of 5).
  - This may signal the market is expensive or crowded.
- If too many stocks qualify:
  - Rank by expected earnings yield (E/P).
  - Exclude those with suspiciously high yields (>35%), which often indicate problems.
  - Or prioritize stocks with the best fundamental scores.
- For most retail investors:
  - 50 stocks is too much.
  - Aim for 25 or even 10 if managing < $50,000.
  - Diversify so no sector exceeds 25% of your portfolio.
- If time is limited, 5 well-chosen stocks in different sectors may be enough.

Final Advice

- Adjust the strategy to suit your **risk tolerance** and **available time**.
- Always **paper-trade** first.
- If you have historical data, **back-test** and **tune** the approach.
- Expect lower returns in live trading than in backtests, but thoughtful adaptation can keep the strategy relevant.

Links

https://www.youtube.com/watch?v=zlYJ1eRjXvA

https://www.youtube.com/watch?v=uGUlUg_617o

20   Short Squeeze

A **short squeeze** happens when a heavily shorted stock rises sharply because short sellers are forced to buy shares to cover their positions. This buying pressure can drive the price even higher.

I look for short squeeze candidates using Finviz.com. I use a **short float threshold of 35%**. But keep in mind: high short interest often exists for good reason (pending lawsuits, deteriorating sales, etc.). So always choose stocks with **strong fundamentals**.

Example Results
Paper-trade tests (as of 9/4/15):

Stock	Buy Date	Return	Annualized	SPY return
CALM	07/16/15	-3%	-33%	-1%
GME	07/16/15	-1%	-7%	-1%

The following are real trades as of 09/04/15.

Stock	Buy Date	Return	Sold date
CALM	03/11/15	47%	N/A
GME	04/06/15	8%	N/A

Case Study: Cal-Maine Foods (CALM)

CALM fell from over $60 to about $46, which made it a strong candidate for me. On 12/15/2015, its opening price was $46.76.

Why buy a falling stock?
Because the story wasn't over. It had **solid fundamentals** and was heavily shorted (short float >55%). That setup offered explosive potential if sentiment changed. Here's how I analyzed it.

Screening and Technical Indicators
CALM passed my **Short Screen**, which looks for:
- **Short float >35%** and
- **Strong fundamentals**.

Most stocks with high short interest deserve it—but for CALM, I found no clear justification for the extreme bearishness.

Technical snapshot on 12/15/2015 (from Finviz.com):

	Condition	Indicate	12/15/2015
Short Float	>35%	Short squeeze	55%
RSI(14)	<30%	Oversold	31%
SMA-20	<0	Short-term down	-13%
SMA-50	<0	Mid-term down	-17%
SMA-200	<0	Long-term down	-9%
Recom.	1 - Buy & 5 – Sell	3 – Neutral	2

Interpretation:
Technically, it was deeply oversold and trending down—typical for short squeeze setups.

Fundamentally speaking
Did this stock deserve this hatred? From the following table, it is a big NO.

	Condition	Indicate	12/15/2015
Forward P/E	>0 and < 20	Favorable	7
ROE	>20%	Favorable	40%
Profit Margin	>8%	Favorable	15%
EPS Q/Q	>15%	Favorable	418%
Sales Q/Q	>10%	Favorable	71%
P/FCF	<15	Favorable	12
Debt / Equity	<.5 (industry related)	Favorable	.05

Almost every metric was outstanding. One or two positives wouldn't be enough to buy—but across the board, the fundamentals screamed **Buy**.

My Scoring Systems

I used three proprietary scoring systems plus PEY (Pow's Earnings Yield):

System	Passing Score	CALM Score
P-Score	3	6
Short-Term Score	15	40
Long-Term Score	15	24
PEY	5%	23%

Notes:
- **P-Score** uses free Finviz metrics plus Fidelity Analyst Opinions. Detailed in my book *Scoring Stocks*.
- **Short-Term and Long-Term Scores** use extra metrics and paid sources. I regularly adjust them.
- **PEY (Pow's Earnings Yield)** is my version of EV/EBIT. PEY > 20% is excellent.

When a stock scores this high across the board, I get cautious—it almost seems *too* good. But my checks revealed no hidden problems.

Intangibles
- Articles on Seeking Alpha raised no red flags.
- Bird flu risk was low thanks to controlled farming.
- Egg prices were normalizing, which might lower EPS a bit. But with a forward P/E under 7 and PEY over 23%, the downside risk was limited.

Scenarios I considered:
- Another bird flu outbreak (elsewhere) would *boost* egg prices and CALM's profits.
- Even if CALM itself faced an outbreak, impact would be localized, with management prepared to contain it.
- Overseas outbreaks (e.g., in China) could shift demand to US producers like CALM.

Bonus Metrics (from GuruFocus, paid)
- **F-Score:** 7 (favorable)
- **Z-Score:** 8 (favorable)

Summary
Technically weak, fundamentally strong.

It might continue drifting down, but when it turns, the move up could be dramatic.

Most value stocks need patience. You're swimming against the tide until the market recognizes real value.

No one can perfectly call the bottom. But I expected a short squeeze when short sellers struggled to find shares. Rising interest rates could also force covers. Plus, they were paying an ~8% dividend—shorting such stocks is expensive.

My bet: **Low risk, high upside.**

Result:

I bought on 3/11/15 and sold on 10/28/15 for a **48% gain (77% annualized)**.

Links

Timing: https://www.youtube.com/watch?v=XexaKTJ-qQU
Short squeeze: https://www.youtube.com/watch?v=XAyaQaWajpl
https://www.youtube.com/watch?v=T5MmthJgwSU

#Filler: No Such Thing as a Free Lunch

You've probably seen those YouTube ads: "Follow our stock picks and get rich!" They'll highlight winners like Apple or Amazon—conveniently leaving out the losers that flopped or went bankrupt.

The same goes for flashy trading systems. They look amazing—until you realize the backtests quietly excluded all the failed stocks. That's called *survivorship bias*—and it paints a misleading picture.

In this book, I won't sell you dreams. The strategies here are built for the long haul and rooted in real-world experience—not marketing hype.

Because if guaranteed money-making systems really existed... we wouldn't have poor people, would we?

21   Year-end strategies

I use two main strategies for the year-end period:
1. **Buy the Year-End Winners (YEW):**
    This approach rides the "window dressing" effect, where institutional investors buy well-performing stocks to make their portfolios look better. It worked in many years, but not in 2018—so I skipped it in 2019.
2. **Buy the Year-End Losers (YEL):**
    This strategy takes advantage of tax-loss selling. Investors dump losing positions before year-end for tax purposes. I look for **value stocks** among these beaten-down names— but avoid companies at real risk of bankruptcy. This strategy worked well for me in 2018, so I continued using it in 2019.

How to Backtest These Strategies
If you have access to a historical database, here's how you can design and test variations of these strategies:
- **Define start dates:**
    - For winners: test 9/1, 10/1, and 11/1.
    - For losers: test 12/1 and 12/15.
- **Define holding periods:**
    - Test 1, 2, 3, and 6 months.
- **Choose your testing period:**
    - I recommend starting with data from 2000 onward. Avoid data before 1995 since market structure was different.
    - Personally, I often test just the last 3 years for speed.
- **Benchmark against SPY or the S&P 500 index.**
- **Use annualized returns for comparisons.**
- **Handle missing data:**
    - If a date is a holiday or weekend, use the next trading day.
- **Clean your universe:**
    - Exclude penny stocks, illiquid foreign companies, extreme dividend payers, or stocks returning capital, which can distort results.
- **Sort using different metrics:**
    - For example, Expected Earnings Yield (E/P) or composite scores.
    - Test using the top 2–5 stocks per sort.

- **Track maximum drawdowns:**
  - For example, I once had a -52% drawdown from 12/1/2007 to 12/1/2008, followed by a 256% rebound the next year.
- **Manually check results with negative returns** to avoid formula errors.

General Screening Notes
- For **Year-End Winner** strategies:
  - Focus on large-cap stocks with strong year-to-date gains, which are typical window-dressing targets.
- For **Year-End Loser** strategies:
  - Seek small-cap stocks with large losses (>50% YTD), but ensure they're still profitable (>15% profit margins).
  - Avoid stocks that are "deserved losers" heading to bankruptcy.
- In my testing, **profitable small caps often outperform** other groups.

Example Historical Results

Strategy	Start Date	Duration	Avg. Annualized Return	Max Drawdown
YE Winners	10/1	4 months	40%	-36%
YE Losers	12/1	6 months	42%	-28%

Observations from Past Years
2015:
My YEL screens were weaker. Many low-scoring stocks were foreign companies with questionable financials and many were energy companies (I was already overexposed).
- Many had Expected Earnings Yields >35% but also Debt/Equity >1.
- Even when historically profitable, I skipped many that year given the risks.

Lesson: Adjust strategies to market conditions.

My Approach in 2018
- **Market environment:** Risky.

- o I didn't buy winners. Instead, I shorted selected losers.
- **Year-End Losers:**
  - o Bought between Nov. 1–Dec. 31.
  - o Criteria: profitable (>15% margins), big losers (typically >50% decline), small-cap preference.
- I adapted to volatility by buying dips (defined as ~5% down from recent highs) and selling short-term bounces (~5% from recent lows).

Selling rules depend on context and are not included here.
I base all these on thorough historical testing. But every market is different. Even the best research needs adjustment.

Key point: Over time, the better educated you are, the higher your odds of success.

Example Results
2018 Year-End Trade Performance
- Best monthly result ever:
  - o Average purchase date: 12/27/2018
  - o Valuation date: 1/28/2019
  - o Return: **53% in a month (~648% annualized)**

Note: Such extreme returns are unlikely to repeat every year, but the process itself is valuable.
I also adjust quantity (Q=1) to simplify tracking. Stocks with multiple purchases were normalized for analysis.

I sold YRCW on its earnings date if earnings were positive. I recommend always cancelling open orders before earnings releases.

As of 9/7/2019:
- LCI was up 185%.
- YRCW was down 27%, but one retirement account position sold for ~100% gain.

2019 Year-End Performance
I didn't hit 50% in a month but still achieved strong results:

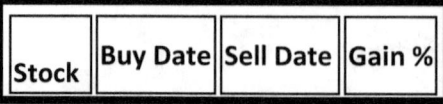

Stock	Buy Date	Sell Date	Gain %

Stock	Buy Date	Sell Date	Gain %
HOFT	12/04/19	01/14/20	4%
HOFT	12/06/19	01/15/20	11%
METC	12/03/19	01/02/20	14%
REI	12/09/19	01/03/20	35%
EGY	12/10/19	–	25%
SND	12/10/19	–	0%
SBOW	12/17/19	–	-19%
SD	12/17/19	–	-17%
URBN	12/20/19	–	3%
GT	12/11/19	–	-8%
CAL	12/11/19	–	-4%

- Portfolio average (11 stocks): ~4.7% over ~1 month.
- SPY benchmark for same period: ~3.87%.
- Beat SPY by ~19%.

Narrower selection (4 stocks with Earnings Yield >20%):

- Return: ~10%.

2018 Longer-Term Holding Test Example

I also analyzed optimal hold periods for 2018 purchases (assuming a uniform 12/27/2018 buy date):

Holding Period	Annualized Return	SPY Annualized
1 month	497%	72%
2 months	366%	74%
3 months	178%	52%
5 months	17%	31%

Lesson: historically, 6 months gave the best balance, but I often take quicker profits in volatile markets.

2020 Example

Data from my book *Best Stocks for 2021*, measured from 12/10/2020 to ~1/9/2021:

Symbol	Return	Annualized
BCOR	20%	224%
CEPU	-10%	-114%
EEX	-8%	-94%
FANG	17%	191%
STFC	9%	105%

- Portfolio average: 5% (~63% annualized).
- SPY: ~3% (~37% annualized).
- Beat SPY by ~48%.

Closing Advice
- Markets evolve, so always test and adapt your approach.
- The best strategy in one year may fail the next if conditions change.
- Avoid blindly repeating past methods without testing them in current market contexts.

Bottom line:
Do the work, stay flexible, and keep learning to improve your odds over the long run.

22   Rocket stocks

Certain stocks repeatedly hit new yearly highs and can keep surging for a while, seemingly defying fundamental valuation rules. For example, Tesla gained about 400% between April and October 2013. But when these momentum trends break, the losses can be brutal: BlackBerry (BBRY) soared roughly 30× over five years, then lost 95% of its value over the next four.

These "rocket stocks" often:
- Have new, disruptive products that capture market excitement.
- Are sometimes targets of institutional investor manipulation.
- Collapse quickly if they face unfixable issues like intense competition or major lawsuits.

They can rise like rockets—and fall just as fast.

Common Characteristics of Rocket Stocks
My testing suggests these stocks often share a few traits:

- Trading at or near **52-week highs** (easy to find on financial news sites or links like Barchart's 52-week highs).
- **SMA-50 > SMA-200** (both available for free on sites like Finviz.com), signaling upward trends.
- Stock price typically over $10.
- Market capitalization often between **$3 billion and $8 billion**:
  - Institutional investors tend to favor this range.
  - I also look at $100 million–$500 million companies for higher potential upside (though they're riskier).
- Listed on one of the **three major U.S. exchanges**.
- Trading volume at least **double the average**, confirming buying pressure.
- High ratings or strong timing grades on various investing sites (some free).

You can adapt these criteria depending on sector. For example, small-cap biotech or tech companies might not fit standard filters but can still behave like rocket stocks.

Insider Buying and Avoiding Traps
- Insider purchases can be a strong positive signal.
- Always **avoid companies heading toward bankruptcy**, no matter how high they're surging.

Selling Discipline: Managing Greed
Don't get greedy. Rocket stocks often give back all their gains—and more—when the momentum fades or institutional investors rotate into the next hot sector.

Key tactic:
- Use mental (a.k.a. trailing) stops—e.g., 10% below the most recent high.
- When the stock drops 10% below your last stop level, sell immediately without regret.

My testing suggests an **average holding period of ~3 months** works best. But remember—some rocket stocks defy gravity longer than you expect. No one can consistently time exact tops and bottoms.

Important rule: Never buy a growth stock that is in a confirmed downtrend.

FAANG Stocks: A Case Study in Rocket-Like Behavior

FAANG (Facebook/Meta, Amazon, Apple, Netflix, Google) stocks are often seen as defining the market itself. But as a more conservative investor, I see them differently.

For cap-weighted ETFs like SPY, FAANG stocks have outsized influence. They performed brilliantly over some periods, but also experienced massive declines when momentum reversed.

Below is historical data (all estimates, no dividends or fees included) illustrating their rocket-like rise and fall.

FAANG Historical Returns (Selected Periods)

Stock	Price on 8/5/17	8/16–8/17 Return	8/17–8/18	8/18–10/18	1/3/22–1/3/23
FB	169.62	37%	7%	-84%	-63%
AMZN	173.85	29%	88%	2%	-50%
AAPL	156.39	48%	30%	48%	-31%
NFLX	180.27	48%	94%	-4%	-51%
GOOGL	945.79	17%	33%	-47%	-39%
Average	—	44%	50%	-17%	-47%
SPY	—	14%	15%	5%	-20%

Notes:
- "Beat SPY" for 8/16–8/17 = (44% - 14%) / 14% ≈ 214%.
- Similarly calculated for other periods.

Takeaway: Using trailing stops would have helped avoid much of the ~50% average loss in 2022.

Example Fundamentals (as of 8/5/2017)

Stock	P/E	Fwd P/E	P/S	P/B	Debt/Equity	Sales Q/Q	EPS Q/Q	ROE
FB	37	26	15	7	0.00	45%	69%	23%
AMZN	16	14	6	4	1.11	2%	18%	27%
AAPL	18	15	4	6	0.73	5%	10%	35%
NFLX	221	90	8	25	1.55	32%	58%	13%

Stock	P/E	Fwd P/E	P/S	P/B	Debt/Equity	Sales Q/Q	EPS Q/Q	ROE
GOOGL	34	24	7	4	0.03	21%	-28%	14%
Average	65	34	8	9	0.68	21%	25%	22%
SPY	25	—	2	3	—	—	—	—

Approximate values. Small variations may exist from other sources.

Example Technicals (as of 8/5/2017)

Stock	SMA50%	SMA200%	RSI(14)	52-Week High Diff	Short%	Insider Trans.
FB	8%	23%	67	-3%	1%	-86%
AMZN	35%	8%	51	-6%	1%	0%
AAPL	5%	17%	63	-2%	1%	-31%
NFLX	10%	26%	59	-6%	6%	-69%
GOOGL	-2%	8%	41	-6%	0%	0%
Average	11%	16%	56	-5%	2%	-37%

Interpretation:
- SMA50 and SMA200 trends were generally positive at that time, indicating technical strength even if fundamentals varied.

Summary and Recommendations

FAANG stocks have often been **technically strong but fundamentally expensive**. While they helped drive market returns, they also showed how quickly rocket stocks can crash when momentum fades.

Key recommendations for rocket stocks (including FAANG):
- Use **trailing stops** (e.g., 10% below recent highs) to protect gains.
- Don't cling to them once they become **technically unsound** (e.g., breaking below SMA-20).
- Be cautious with very high P/E ratios (e.g., over 35) unless you have a compelling reason to hold them.
- Remember: even the best rocket stocks can "return to earth" at alarming speeds.

When the narrative is fully priced in, any bad news can cause a violent revaluation.

Bottom line: Enjoy the ride up—but always have an exit plan.

23   Small caps vs. big caps

Small-cap and large-cap stocks rotate in and out of favor depending on market conditions. Sometimes small caps outperform; other times, large caps lead.

Benchmarks:
- Small caps: *Russell 2000* (ETF: **IWM**)
- Large caps: *Russell 1000* (ETF: **IWB**)

Every year, many strong small-cap companies graduate into large-cap status, and weaker large caps can drift down. One simple, practical method to assess the market's preference:

☑ If one ETF consistently outperforms the other over **1 month** and **3 months**, it's a sign that the market currently favors that category.

You can apply the same approach to **value vs. growth** stocks: compare the performance of value-stock ETFs against growth-stock ETFs over the same periods.

This rotation between **small/large** and **value/growth** is a core part of **sector rotation** investing.

Why small-cap growth stocks (<$5 billion market cap) can outperform:
1. It's much easier for a $5 billion company to double than a $50 billion company.
2. Many institutional investors don't pay much attention to sub-$5 billion companies, leaving opportunities for individual investors.

#Filler: Beyond the Unemployment Rate
The headline jobless figure ignores people who've stopped looking, and median incomes are still below 2007 levels. College grads stuck in unrelated jobs—and the global hiring arbitrage—mean many pockets aren't seeing real wage gains.

#Filler: Tesla: Not as "Green" as You Think
An $80K electric car still relies on taxpayer subsidies and creates its own environmental headaches—old batteries in landfills, rare-earth mining, and grid strain. Innovation is vital, but let's be honest about costs and impacts.

24   An aggressive strategy

Below is an outline of an aggressive approach I use, combining screens, vendor data, and my own analysis. Remember: **there are no guarantees.**

Main Steps
1 Market timing—when to buy and sell
2 Screening for candidate stocks
3 Adapting the screen to current market conditions
4 Fundamental scoring
5 Intangible analysis
6 Qualitative analysis
7 Optional: technical analysis

---

1. Market Timing
See the dedicated chapters in this book for details. Timing the broader market helps improve your odds.

---

2. Screening Stocks
Most small caps are under-researched by Wall Street. This makes it possible to discover overlooked gems.
General rules:
- Avoid problematic sectors/countries: banks, lenders, miners, generic-drug makers (branded biotech is fine), insurance companies, and many emerging markets (e.g., China, India, Mexico).
- Exclude firms showing bankruptcy warning signs:
  - Very high debt.
  - Massive insider selling.
  - Weak free cash flow (harder to manipulate than earnings).
  - Poor profit and sales growth vs. prior quarter.

Typical screening criteria (U.S. markets):
- Listed on one of the 3 major U.S. exchanges.
- Market cap between **$200 million and $800 million**.
- Share price **$2–$20**.
- Average daily volume **>8,000 shares** (some use 10,000).
- Short interest **<15%** (some use 10%).
- Expected earnings yield (E/P) **5%–30%**.
- Price **above its 200-day simple moving average (SMA-200)**—a sign of an upward trend.

All of these criteria are easily checked on **Finviz.com**.

☑ Also consider broker tools like **Fidelity's Equity Summary Score** (skip anything <6).

3. Industry/Sector Comparisons

Compare candidates against their industry averages:

- Price/Cash Flow
- Debt levels
- P/E ratio (and its own 5-year average)
- Price/Sales, etc.

4. Sorting the Screened List

☑ Too few stocks? The market may be too risky. Consider relaxing filters.

☑ Too many? Tighten criteria or sort by **expected earnings yield** to prioritize the best.

5. Matching the Market's Preference

If the market favors growth:

- Sort by SMA percentage (50-day or 200-day, depending on your time frame).
- Or use growth metrics like quarter-over-quarter EPS growth.
- Be cautious of stocks with very high SMA % (could signal an unsustainable peak).
- Check **RSI(14)** to avoid overbought names.

If the market favors value:

- Sort by **expected earnings yield (E/P)**.

6. Qualitative Analysis

Most of the above is quantitative. Don't forget to check:

- Business model strength.
- Competitive advantages.
- Management quality.
- Insider buying trends.

☑ Use screens to narrow the universe to a manageable shortlist for deeper review.

7. Screening Tools

Many sites offer screening tools, including built-in strategies.

- **Free:** Finviz.com, Fidelity.com, Yahoo! Finance.
- **Paid/advanced:** AAII, Stock123, Zacks, VectorVest, Validea, GuruFocus.

☑ Backtesting tools help see how screens would have performed historically.

☑ Vendor example: Validea offers prebuilt "guru" strategies.

Examples of Interesting Screens

- "Guru" screens simulating famous investors like Buffett (watch for crowded trades).
- IPO pipeline: companies not on major exchanges a year ago but now moving up.
- Low PEG ratio (<1)—classic growth strategy.
- Momentum: stocks rising over the last 3 months.
- Relative-value: better metrics than industry peers.
- Combined **Growth + Value** ("Growth at a Reasonable Price").
- M&A candidates (small firms with unique tech or markets).
- Candidates for major exchange listings (forcing ETFs to buy them).
- Contrarian: buy last year's big losers if fundamentally sound.
- Top-down: focus on best-performing sectors/industries.
- Earnings revisions: especially before earnings reports.
- High insider buying.
- Dividend growth stocks (popular in low-rate environments).

☑ Garbage in, garbage out. Be cautious of unreliable financial data, especially from many emerging markets. Always check company profiles and skip those you don't trust.

☑ Fidelity's predefined screens: http://research2.fidelity.com/fidelity/screeners/commonstock/strategies.asp

☑ GuruFocus.com also offers "guru" screens.

Backtesting Considerations

If your screener doesn't include a historical database, you can still test by tracking a virtual portfolio over six months.

Pitfalls to watch for:

1. **Survivorship bias**: Many databases omit delisted/bankrupt stocks. That falsely inflates backtest results.
2. **Human bias**: Investors often buy high, sell low. Sticking to a disciplined strategy helps.

3. **Using the wrong screen** for the current market (e.g., value screens in strong uptrends).
4. **Changing market conditions**: What worked before might stop working.

Example: Low P/E foreign stocks did well before 2010, but not in 2011–2014.

Conclusion

The four steps of investing are: 1. Market Timing, 2. Screening, 3. Analysis and 4. When and what to sell.

Links

- Fidelity's Predefined screens.
http://research2.fidelity.com/fidelity/screeners/commonstock/strategies.asp?

SA article:
(http://seekingalpha.com/article/1806542-a-dividend-portfolio-built-using-the-piotroski-f-score

25 A turnaround strategy for value stocks

Value stocks often remain undervalued for extended periods. But when a turnaround begins, these stocks can deliver substantial profits.

Market Timing
Avoid buying any stock when overall market conditions are risky (as discussed elsewhere in this book). In fact, in those environments you should focus on reducing exposure rather than adding new positions.

Suggested Metrics for Screening
Here's a sample framework you can adapt to your own risk tolerance.

Metric	Base	Conservative	Aggressive
General			
Market Cap	> $300M	> $1B	> $100M
Price	> $2	> $10	> $1
Average Volume	> 20,000	> 50,000	> 10,000
Geography	USA only	USA only	Foreign firms listed in USA
Fundamental			
Forward P/E	< 15	< 10	< 25
Earnings Growth Q/Q	> 5%	> 8%	> 3%
ROE	> 10	> 15	> 5
Price / Free Cash Flow (P/FCF)	< 10	< 8	< 15
Debt / Equity	< 0.5	< 0.25	< 1
Technical			
SMA-50	> 10	> 15	> 5
Miscellaneous			
Blue-Chip/Growth Rating	A or B	A	A or B

Metric	Base	Conservative	Aggressive
Fidelity Rating	> 6	> 8	> 5
IBD Rating	> 60	> 90	> 50
VectorVest Score	≥ 1	≥ 0.8	≥ 1.2
Value Line 3–5 Yr Projection	> 5%	> 10%	> 5%
Zacks Rating	≥ 4	5	≥ 4
ASSS Score (personal system)	≥ 2	≥ 5	≥ 2

Note: These assignment values are only guidelines. Feel free to adjust them to match your own level of risk tolerance. Below, I explain how and why to use them.

Notes on Screening and Adjustments

- **Market Cap and Price**: Finviz (free version) doesn't allow precise ranges—use "Any" and filter manually. Conservative investors target larger, more stable companies; aggressive investors may choose smaller, riskier firms with higher potential upside.
- **Geography**: Prefer U.S.-listed companies. Avoid small firms from developing markets unless you trust their reporting.
- **Forward P/E**: More meaningful than trailing P/E, but confirm positive earnings.
- **Earnings Growth (Q/Q)**: Should be positive, except in deep recessions.
- **ROE**: Measures management efficiency.
- **P/FCF** and **Debt/Equity**: Low values reduce bankruptcy risk.
- **SMA-50**: Helps avoid value traps by selecting stocks starting to rise.
- **Miscellaneous ratings**: Many providers rate stocks based on their systems. Access might require subscriptions, free trials, or even your local library.
- **ASSS**: My personal scoring system. Test it and refine it to suit your approach.

Practical Example

On 10/28/2016, using these criteria, I screened 35 stocks—too many to evaluate deeply.

☑ Suggested approach:
- Sort by Forward P/E (or P/E if needed) in **ascending** order.

- Exclude any stocks with P/E < 2.
- Select your top 10 for deeper analysis.

If you can't find 10 solid candidates, consider waiting. Sometimes market conditions just don't favor value screens.

Qualitative Analysis

Once you have your shortlist:
- Dig into company reports and analyst write-ups.
- Read as many articles as possible about the stock.
- Make sure you understand the business, management, and industry trends.

☑ **Buying tips:**
- For large-cap stocks in calm markets (daily moves <0.5%), market orders work fine.
- If rebuying a stock sold at a loss, wait **31 days** to avoid the **Wash Sale** penalty.

Staying Informed

- Check company news monthly.
- Use a portfolio tracker (e.g., SeekingAlpha.com) to receive alerts and articles about your holdings.

When to Sell

- Re-evaluate your positions every **6 months**.
- If a stock no longer meets your criteria—or the overall market is turning risky—consider selling.
- Be mindful of taxes:
  - If close to qualifying for **long-term capital gains**, consider waiting to sell winners.
  - Sell losers immediately for tax-loss harvesting.

☑ **Portfolio management tip:**
After selling, rebalance your portfolio for proper diversification by sector and market cap.

Top-Down Approach

This approach can work in parallel:
- Identify strong-performing sectors (e.g., using **Finviz.com's** sector performance tools).
- Drill down to find the best stocks within those sectors.
- Many brokers (like Fidelity) also provide sector-relative metrics.

Real-World Example:
My Recommended Stocks That Were Acquired/Delisted

Turnaround and value strategies often lead to buyout targets, especially after market crashes.

Stock	Recommended Date	Delisted Date	Days Held	Total Return	Annualized Return
USAK	12/15/21	09/14/22	273	79%	105%
BDSI	12/15/21	03/22/22	97	116%	436%
CTB	02/08/21	06/17/22	129	15%	41%
Average	-	-	71	70%	194%

These outcomes demonstrate why value investing in turnarounds can be highly rewarding—though you need patience and a solid strategy.

#Filler: Golden Doom
With today's massive military spending, can we really stop hypersonic missiles from our adversaries? The cost of launching one missile versus intercepting it might be so lopsided that defense becomes unsustainable.

Maybe the smartest strategy... is avoiding war altogether.

Section IV: Miscellaneous

26 Institutional investors

Institutional investors include banks, hedge funds, insurance companies and mutual funds. They are important as they move the market, not the retail investors.

You want to follow them closely. When they buy specific stocks, buy the same stocks and vice versa. It is better to be one step before their actions. Due to their large holdings, usually it takes more than a week to finish the trade. Basically this is how day traders make money by jumping onto their wagons. When you see a sudden surge in volume of a specific stock, there is a good chance the institutional investors are trading.

Several sites including GuruFocus.com keep track of the stocks they are holding and their current trades. Finviz.com has similar information. IBD gives higher ratings to the stocks that are held by institutional investors.

Normally the stocks owned by the institutional investors have larger market caps (over 5 billion) and most have stock prices over $10. It takes days or even weeks to trade a stock due to their large holding, and that is how day traders take advantage of it.

Once in a while, their trades are not rational. When you act against them, you need a good reason and be patient.

I took advantage of them using Apple for illustration:

- Recommended in my book Scoring Stocks to buy Apple in June, 2013 (the publish date) while most of the institutional investors were dumping Apple. Apple scored very high in my book then.
- I recommended selling Apple in my blog in Feb., 2015 when Apple was $132. The profit is about $60 per share from the recommended dates.
- I took advantage of the correction making 12% in 2015 for holding Apple for about 2 months.

27   Follow the trend

Many sectors are affected by the aging population such as health insurance, drug companies, health care delivery… I had a great year in drug companies in 2014 but not that great in 2015.

Common sense is the best way to look at specific sectors and follow with a thorough analysis. As of 09/24/2015, the following were my holdings including sold stocks in my taxable account in 2015.

Health insurance stocks:

Stock	Buy Date	Sold Date	Return	Annualized
AET	10/15/14	N/A	59%	63%
CI	10/15/14	N/A	63%	67%

Video game stocks:

The video game industry is thriving too as we spend a lot of our time playing video games. It is very expensive to produce a franchise video game, so it will be limited to a few companies. The franchise video games have their product cycle. GLUU produces games for mobile devices. They have a deal with a Chinese company to dip into that huge market. Game Stop may not be a good one long-term as most games will be delivered on-line by-passing the retail stores.

Stock	Buy Date	Sold Date	Return	Annualized
EA	03/26/15	N/A	23%	45%
EA	03/26/15	N/A	23%	45%
GLUU	01/28/15	N/A	32%	48%
TTWO	10/08/13	01/05/15	59%	47%
TTWO	10/07/13	01/05/15	63%	50%

TTWO	09/11/13	01/05/15	64%	48%

GLUU is more risky than the others and that is why I only had one purchase. The annualized returns are in a similar range.

EA and TTWO are not the largest video game companies. I wish they would be acquired to boost up my profits.

I have two more purchases on TTWO that I gave to my grandchildren and they are not listed here. I bet they are stable and growing companies for the long term. While my grandchildren are playing the games, I hope they know they're also the owners of the company.

28   Tech stocks in the last 20 years

I tried to use my historical database to test out the NASDAQ 100. The return was great. To illustrate, from 1/4/1999 to 6/6/2001, the annualized return is 54% vs SPY's 1.6% without considering dividends. Do not 'wow' too early. One reason for the high performance is due to the survivor bias. Many internet companies were taken out from the index and/or the database, and hence the performance as a group is deceivingly high.

The following chart is for the popular high-tech companies for the selected 10 years. For every one of the following successful high-tech companies, there must be many that do not make it.

	1990-2000	2000-2010
	Annualized Return	Annualized Return
Microsoft	940%	-4%
EMC	7500%	-7%
Apple	20%	65%
Dell	8200%	-7%
Average	**4000%**	**12%**

The above figures are estimates for demonstration purposes without considering dividends and compounding. Dell has been privatized today. Now, we can draw some conclusions.

- Tech stocks usually beat the S&P 500 index. Risk usually pays.
- 1990-2000 are the golden years for tech stocks.
- 2000-2010 are not so good for tech stocks due to the crash of 2000. If it were not for Apple, the return of this portfolio would be negative.
- Except with Apple, it indicates the first ten years (or the early phase) of the tech stocks gave us the best returns. After they become mature companies, they seldom maintain the same growth rates. The worst of the group in the first 10 years became the best after 2000.

Buy when the market does not favor this sector
Interestingly, you should buy when the institutional investors are dumping, such as buying Apple in May, 2013 as recommended in my book Scoring Stocks. Ensure they have value first by scoring them fundamentally and allow at least one year for the market to recognize the values. I reviewed my old blog and found some bargains I described on 12/03/2012. Here is the performance summary. Again, all performance returns are annualized.

The stocks are AAPL, CSCO, INTC, MSFT, XRX, STX, WDC and ALU.

	One year later	Two years later
Ann. Return	84%	59%
SPY Ann. Return	28%	23%
Beat SPY by	200%	157%

Interestingly, AAPL is the weakest performer in both tests. It must start with a high price.

29   Many small fish or a few big fish

Do you want to buy many stocks or just concentrate on a few stocks?

There are advantages and disadvantages for both. Interestingly, the advantage of one strategy is the disadvantage of the other. I'm speaking from my own experiences.

Before 2012, I bought more stocks at smaller amounts than today. Besides diversification, I enjoyed a larger database to monitor my performances on many screens and the metrics I used. Virtual trading could achieve the same performance monitors. However, real trading is quite different as it does not include how we actually trade. I would not learn seriously the lessons from virtual trading such as losing all my money in one stock. We cannot avoid losing money but some can be avoided and/or we can reduce our losses.

From 2012 on, I doubled most of my buys except the risky ones. I even place two orders on the same stock with one almost at the market price. For some really good stocks, I even bought 3 times my average purchase.

The changes are due to:

1. I cannot find too many good stocks.
2. I do not have time to follow so many stocks.
3. I find some marginally sound stocks that may not perform and/or they are risky.

It turns out that my total return is better than my previous return and I spend less time investing.

Filler: The world is round, honey

My spouse complained I made the wrong turn. I replied eventually we would be right as the world is round. Time wise I was wrong but logic wise I was right.

30   Secular market

In a secular bull market, there is greater profit potential in growth stocks especially the momentum stocks than value stocks. The industrial commodities and oil industries will generally outperform the overall market in a growing economy.

In a secular bear market, value stocks especially the dividend stocks will generally outperform the overall market. When the government lowers the interest rates to stimulate the economy, timing is important to switch between industries that are sensitive to the interest rate. The value of long-term bonds is inversely proportional to the interest rate. A bond with a low yield will depreciate when the interest rates rise as it is better to buy a new bond yielding higher interest.

There are market cycles within a secular market, so trade according to the current phase of the market cycle. However, be diligent to weigh more on stocks in a secular bull market, and vice versa.

Afterthoughts
- My friend Joseph wrote:

My own discipline is to conduct deep research, buying unloved and undervalued stocks in out-of-favor sectors in which I see a catalyst for change in investor perception and/or in the sector or company's ability to use that change to increase their revenues, market share and margins. I buy the best quality firms anywhere I find them, the less "popular" the area the better (yielding better entry prices,) then hold unless market conditions change, or I find a more compelling investment -- if we are in a secular bull market for example!

But during secular Bears, no matter how exceptional the company, I know their stock can be battered by a general market malaise as well as by a single news item, or event beyond their control. In big "B" Bear markets, people are fickle and will panic at the slightest provocation. So we use the same scrupulous research methodology but we also conduct a daily review of all client accounts and a regular reallocation of assets. Different phases in the market cycle call for different measures.

31   Double down

When you lose 25% on a stock, do you want to buy more, or even double down? Most likely the advice is 'No', but there are exceptions. Find out why it is down and check out the arguments about why it might recover. Here are some of my actual experiences.

- I would average down on CAT, or even double down on CAT. I just bought the company and it lost 10%. CAT did not have a good audience in shorting the stock. It would recover when the economy improved. At this price (about $75 in July, 2012) and its low P/E, it could be hitting the bottom. The institutional investors were selling it like hot cakes. [Update: As of 1/2015, it is $84 and the fundamentals are still great except with the high debt.]

  You need to be patient as you're swimming against the tide. Wait for two or three years for the economy to return.

- Averaging down is about timing.
  Take CROX in the last several years as an example. CROX had a good audience of shorters and it suffered from several temporary setbacks. The chance of losing 50% was about the same as gaining 100% to me at the time I evaluated the company. After one year, it gained over 200% from the bottom. However, averaging down does not always work.

- When doubling down is important. Stay away when the downward momentum is too high and/or there is no good chance of recovering. I had to admit I lost a lot when I doubled down on CROX too early. My 200% gain of CROX did not recover the losses of the trades on this stock due to getting in too early.

  When a stock has been doubled, most likely it is not wise to double your buy (or you call it double up). The reward / risk ratio would usually be decreased. There are exceptions. I prefer to "buy low and sell high" rather than "buy high and sell higher".

  Make sure the setback is temporary and it is supported by good fundamentals. When the stock has a potential to go to zero due to fraud or a big lawsuit pending, it would be a fool's game to double down. Companies sue each other, or are being sued by the government all the time. Identify how serious the lawsuits are.

- Again, timing is everything. No one can determine the bottom of a stock constantly, but we can detect the trend via charts such as SMA-50 (Simple Moving Average of the last 50 trade sessions). Analyze the stock you want to double down on by performing both fundamental analysis and technical analysis.

To conclude, there is no "Yes and No" answer. Your success requires you to do some homework (analyzing the outlook and via charts) and sometimes you need some luck. Most of the time, walking away from a loss is better than having additional losses on the same stock.

Even the best investor makes a mistake once in a while. If the mistake is beyond his/her control, it is not a mistake but just bad luck. Forget it and move on. If the mistake is due to poor analysis, learn from it and never repeat the same mistake. In any case, move on and do not be emotionally attached.

Filler:

- Identify exceptional companies with a durable competitive advantage.
- High taxes have been proven bad for the economy and the stock market throughout our history.
- As Gandhi said, the world has enough resources for all but we're not unselfish enough to share.

Filler: Golden Gate

Just minutes ago, my mail system asked me to sign in. I did and repeatedly they asked me to sign in again and again. I closed down everything and followed Gates' golden rule: If everything does not work, just power down everything and power it up again. I did this and prayed too. It works. Thanks Gates for fixing my problem.

There is NO one doing BASIC quality control. If it happened in my generation, many guys would be fired. Mediocrity is the new norm?

32   Adaptive strategy

What is the best metric for evaluating stocks? Most people will tell you P/E. I use estimated earnings (E) and P/E becomes Forward P/E (a.k.a. Expected P/E). Switch it over to E/P for easier to understand, and it is termed Earnings Yield (EY = P/E). However, the 'E' is not 'expected' which is better to predict future stock value. I prefer EY to be calculated with Forward Earnings and most sites do not provide it but you can calculate it easily.

When the market favors momentum stocks, fundamental stocks even with good Earnings Yields may not work. In this case, I prefer momentum stocks with EY better than average.

EV/EBITDA (obtainable from Yahoo!Finance) is better than P/E as it includes interest, debt and cash. Switch it over and it is True Earnings Yield (my term).

Some may tell you ROI and there is a successful book on ROI.

Both P/E and ROI should not be the only metric as there is no single evergreen metric. That is why most people have poor performance by following them blindly. It is the herd theory: The performance is usually decreased in the longer term when too many folks follow it.

Here is my test on the S&P 500 stocks from April 1, 2019 to July 1, 2019.
I used the top 10 stocks from each sort. Commissions, dividends and spreads are omitted for simplicity. SPY's return is annualized to 13.8%.

Value parameters

Top 10 stocks sorted by	Best SPY[1]
EY in descending order	-251%
Dividend Yield in descending order	-291%[2]

Opposite of the above

Top 10 stocks sorted by	Best SPY[1]
EY in ascending order	6%
Dividend Yield = 0	138%[3]

[1] Beat by % = (Avg. return of 10 stocks – SPY) / SPY
[2] Including dividend yields for the average 10 stocks and SPY, "Beat SPY' is reduced to -241%.

[3] Just randomly picked the 10 stocks that do not pay dividends as there are more stocks with no dividends.

33   A planned strategy

This strategy is planned today (3/1/2021). It may not materialize as planned. Study the reasons behind this strategy, and it should work in the long run.

Phase 1. I expect that the market is peaking today, but I could be wrong. Roughly, my portfolio is evenly distributed between Cash, Contra ETFs (PSQ, SH, DOG and some contra ETFs for smaller stocks), commodity (gold, silver, minerals and oil) and Stocks (described in detail) later.

The market could stay in this phase for a long time, and the market seems to be volatile. I will trade them to take advantage of market fluctuations. I would stick with the above allocation as I do not know how long this phase would stay, and I do not expect the market rise at the same rates as in the last 2 years.

There are many ways to detect market crashes, namely via death cross (SMA-20 and SMA-50) and SMA-350. I would add death cross (SMA-50 and SMA-200) and SMA-400. There may be false signals to tell you to exit and return to the market shortly.

Phase 2 Market crash. I would decrease my stock holdings and increase my contra ETFs.

Phase 3 Recover. I would close out all contra ETFs, and increase my stock holdings especially on stocks that would recover faster. Start to close precious metal stocks.

Phase 4. Up. Return to stocks especially technology stocks.

34   "To short" or "Not to short"

In my Best Stocks for 2021 2nd Edition, I had two lists for short-term holding, one to momentum and one for short. Here are the results after a month.

Momentum Stocks (Total count = 7. Date: 02/08/2021. End: 03/08/2021).

Symbol	Name	Return %
ATGE	Adtalem	-1%
ATRS	Antares Pharma	-9%
CMRE	Costamare	11%
REGI	Renewable Energy	-40%
RIO	Rio Tinto ADR	-6%
SPWH	Sportsman's Ware	-1%
WIRE	Encore Wire	8%
	Avg	-5%
	SPY	1%
	Beat SPY by	-916%

Selling Shorts (Total count = 3. Date: 02/08/2021. End: 03/08/2021).

Symbol	Name	Return %
HYLN	Hyliion	17%
NEXT	NextDecade	29%
RMO	Romeo Power	33%
	Avg	26%
	SPY	1%
	Beat SPY by	3833%

The average of these two lists beat SPY by 1458% without considering dividends and fees. This is the return if you invested evenly in these two lists. Past performances have nothing to do with future performances. The investment in my $20 book was trivial compared to what they would gain.

Initially the results were reversed. The performances depend on the market that rose initially and plunged later. I recommend trading the list when the trend is with us. If the market is up 3 sessions in a row, it should be trending up, and hence buy the stocks in the momentum list. Close the positions when the trend is down. If the market is down 3 sessions in a row, short sell the stocks in the Selling Short list. It is a mistake to ignore the trend as some may wonder why s/he buys the stocks that have been up in the last 3 sessions.

35   More on strategies

To me, the most important advance for retail investors is the availability of historical databases at prices we can afford. It shows us the performance of our strategies for the last 10 or so years in an hour or two. The following are my suggestions to make better use of the findings from these databases and their pitfalls.

- Start with proven metrics as demonstrated by research (the metrics used in this book and other sources such as from SSRN.com) and your own trading.
- Select parameters as close to your trading style as possible. For example, if you only deal with small stocks, select market caps from 100 M to 500 M.
- Some screens perform better in the short term while some perform better in the long term. I recommend testing the performances for 3 months, 6 months, 12 months and 18 months for short-term screens (1 month for momentum stocks). If you believe the strategy is for a long term only, get the performances for 6, 12 and 18 months.
- In 2015 (use a date more current), I start with the year 2000 and end with 2014 for a total of 15 sets. It covers the two market cycles. The market before 2000 may not be relevant as today's market is quite different from that time. Actually I prefer the tests for the last 10 years.
- Run the screen in the first part of the year and test the performance at year end. Repeat the test for the rest of the intervals: 3, 6, 12 and 18 (adding 1 for momentum and 2 years for long term).
- I do not start with an amount (say $10,000) and see the results at the end of a period (say 10 years). It could be misleading when your screen performs exceptionally well (or bad) in the first few years. I call the one I use "window testing" for lack of a better term. To illustrate this, the start date is Jan. 1, 2000 (actually Jan. 2 due to holiday) and end date is Jan. 1, 2001. The next set is Feb. 1, 2000 to the start, the next set is Feb. 1, 2001 and so on.
- I use the next available date if the date falls on a weekend or a holiday for consistency. If you have more time, try another set starting in mid-year. For some strategies and when time allows, I test the strategy monthly.
- If my screen makes 10% and the market makes 20%, it is 100% worse off. I compare how much it beats the market.
- For simplicity I use the SPY to simulate the market. No index is ideal. The S&P 500 is capitalization cap weighed. In 2015, the bubble stocks

dominated this index. The better selection is to choose the index according to the type of stocks that you usually have such as the Russell 2000 for small stocks.

- Consider safety such as the <u>Sharpe</u> ratio, maximum drawdown (peak-to-trough loss) and a winning percent. A winning percentage of 55% (target for 52%) is very good. If your strategy has a very high winning percent, most likely it is safe but just not only performing.
- Why your actual performance with real money may be worse than the tested strategy:
  - Survivor bias. Most databases take out the stock when they're bankrupt, merged or acquired. Hence the performance of the screen is better than it really is as there are more bankrupt companies than merged /acquired. From my experience I have at least one such stock in a year. Hence, the test results are not correct if the database does not take care of this bias.
  - Emotions do not allow you to stick with the strategy.
  - The strategy does not work in the current market; that's why we need to test the performance of the last 6 months.
  - There is idle money between trades.
- I use the top 5 stocks (hence sorting is important). In addition, if you do not buy foreign stocks, deselect them. I use the top 2 for some strategies such as sector rotation.
- If you cannot find data in some screens in any month, just leave it blank (actually null), which will not be included in calculating averages / totals. If the market is risky, you may not find any value stocks.
- The most recent tests would resemble the performance of the strategy better. Hence, I have an extra average of performance on more recent tests.
- Return = (B-A)/A, while A is the return of SPY for me. It does not handle the negative numbers. Use (B-A)/ABS(A). In any case, check the results to see they make sense. When B or A is zero or a very small number, the results could be misleading. I usually delete the test results on huge returns in both directions.
- Using sector rotation strategy as an example, the holding periods are 1, 2 and 3 months.
- Some strategies work better on different phases of the market cycle such as growth stocks in the market trending up and staple stocks during market plunges.

36   Miscellaneous strategies

- Some **mutual funds** have been losing a lot of money such as during the internet crash in 2000. Buy those funds (usually sector funds) that you expect them to recover. It could be a tax strategy as they will not distribute profits to their fund owners for a while.

- **Inflation**. They are gold (GLD, gold mines such as RING as an ETF and gold coins / bars) and silver. I prefer skipping copper and other commodities including oil unless the economy is trending up. Bonds and CDs are most likely not good investments as they return you with cash that have been depreciated due to inflation.

- Supply and demand. In 2009 and 2020, the Fed printed a lot of money excessively to save the economy. In the long run, our national debts will increase. In addition, it could cause inflation unless the economy recovers due to the simulation as in 2009. There is a lot of money chasing fixed assets such as gold and stocks. As a result, both of these assets would likely rise, especially in the short term. If we have hyperinflation, we would lose the buying power after cashing in the appreciated stocks.

- Almost **day trading**. When the stock is rising in the morning, there is a better chance it would continue the trend and vice versa. Reverse the trade at around 3 pm, and day traders almost never leave their positions open during weekends and/holidays. The chance is improved if both the market and the sector the stock is in are both rising. Take advantage of institutional investors. When they trade, they need days and even weeks to trade a stock. You can tell from the volume of the trade and usually the stock belongs to blue chips. Join the wagon.

- As stated before, some strategies described in this book work better than the others in different conditions of the market. If you can match the right strategy or strategies, you will see fireworks, and vice versa.

- Index rebalancing. The index such as S&P 500 rebalances at least once a year and some do it 4 times a year. If you buy the stock before it is added to the index, you should make a lot of money. The ETFs that follow the specific index are forced to buy the stocks just added to the index and sell the stocks that have been removed from the index. I do not recommend shorting these stocks, which is risky especially for beginners.

Some indexes provide the criteria to rebalance. Here is my summary from what I guess. It is based on market cap, number of shares floating, the average trading volume (3 to 6 months), how long it has been in the market, profit (better with rising), sales (better with increasing) and any restrictions (such as a foreign stock). There are minor criteria.

I tested a strategy based on the above criteria on S&P 500 for example. First criteria is that the stocks should not be in the index already. So far, the testing has been proved profitable, but the test is too limited.
There are several articles that you can find by googling "Index Rebalance".

- Guru's mistakes. On 4/2021, I had too many contra ETFs betting the market to go down. It did not work due to the excessive supply of USD. I should have followed the market timing such as SMA-400 and/or death cross described in my books. However, if you buy contra ETFs in early 5/2021, you could have made very good money. Shamelessly I assume myself as a 'guru'. There are many similar examples. One analyst shorted the financial services. It did not work initially and he was fired. If the fund let me stay, he could make a fund a lot of money.

- Positioning strategy. Start with two ETFs: SPY (or any ETF that simulates the market) and a money market ETF for example with even positions (i.e., 50% invested in each ETF). At the end of a period (a week or a month depending on how much time you have for investing), reallocate the ETFs as a percentage of how much each ETF gains (i.e., the higher allocation for the winner). For better performance, use more ETFs such as adding QQQ, GLD, SH (contra ETF to SPY) and PSQ (contra ETF to QQQ).

- Buy stocks which are 95% (or 100%) close to 52-week highs. I use Finviz's Screener. To limit the number of screened stocks, I would select NASDAQ for exchange, USA for country and SMA-20 crossed SMA-50. Need to evaluate individual stock. Stop loss and market timing are important as evidenced in 2000.

- If the SMA-50 is above the SMA-100 (both available from Finviz), the stock is considered to be in an uptrend, else down trend. It is safer to use an ETF. Again, use stop orders to protect your trade. I recommend keeping the cash in the down trend instead of shorting. Use at least one more technical indicator to confirm your decision. If you start testing from 2000, you would avoid some losses from the two market crashes (2000 and 2008).

- Follow the rocket. In 2020, they are FAANG. In 2021, they are DogyCoin, GME and AMC. The geniuses are those who follow the uptrend, and the losers are those who do not have an exit strategy such as trailing stops updated every week for rising stocks.

- Market neutral. If you think you are a better investor than others and do not want to time the market, buy a few stocks (say 3) and short sell the same number. Review your performance periodically.

- Guru's mistakes. More than one time, a guru was fired due to betting big on a certain theme, and after a while, his predictions turned out to be correct. We have to evaluate his 'bad', and they could be at fault in time and they could turn out to be gems.

- Most of our strategies buy on momentum and sell when the momentum is reversed. Here is one opposite strategy: buy on increasing value (from fundamental metrics such as P/E), and sell on decreasing value. The trading could be in multiple trades. The logic is the institutional investors switch sectors, and you make profit by steps ahead of them. It worked in 2021, when the tech sector was switched to retail, and then back to the tech sector. It will not work if the sector stays in momentum for longer periods such as years.

https://www.youtube.com/watch?v=MFVmEcRHpnk&t=332s

37   Monitor performances of strategies

Need to monitor the recent performances of your strategies. Do not invest in the strategies that do not perform well recently. It can be done easily with a service (usually costs) that has a historical database. However, most of them do not take care of the survival bias – they take out the stocks from the database when they are delisted, bankrupt or merged. You just create a watchlist.

For example, the watchlist name is "YearEnd 20211215" keeping track of the stocks screened by your year-end strategy on 12/15/2021. Check out the performance from 12/15/2021 to a month later, and compare it to SPY (an ETF simulating the S&P 500 Index). I usually have 3 watchlists: a primary one, one that has deleted the duplicate stocks in the last month and one that I trade. You do not want to waste time in analyzing the stocks that have been evaluated recently. After the screened stocks, analyze them using tools such as Finviz and Fidelity for example ignoring the foreign stocks selectively or high dumping by insiders.

It is possible but more tedious without a historical database such as Finviz and Fidelity. From our example, just save the stocks in a spreadsheet on 12/15/2021 and enter the stock prices a month later. Besides the strategy, you may want to test the performances of individual metrics such as P/E.

38   Execution of a strategy

Be disciplined
You need to execute your strategy in a disciplined way. Set up a trade plan. The best time to buy is when the market is uptrend. It is uptrend when the SMA-20, SMA-50 and SMA-200 are all positive from Finviz.

Your screen from the strategy may have too many stocks. It would be too time-consuming to evaluate too many stocks. You need to narrow your search by:
- Select the top 5 stocks such as EP (E/P for long-term strategies and SMA-50 for momentum strategies).
- Change the criteria.
- Do a quick analysis to discard stocks such as high Debt/Share (for most industries for long-term strategies.

If you cannot find any stock or too few stocks for comparison, either skip this session or relax the search criteria.

Once the system is set up, you only need very little time and effort to execute an order. From Tuesday to Thursday, I spent about an hour to screen stocks and place orders. Every month, I evaluate my positions and strategies. If you are not active investor like me, you can just spend a few hours every month.

39   My best strategies in 2022

About 25 strategies I keep track of their recent performances, the following are my three best-performed strategies. They represent long term, short term and short.

The performances use today's date which is 3/8/2022. As in most of this book, commissions, dividends and fees are not included. Again, it is for educational purposes only.

In most cases, the stocks are screened by the strategy related screen and further evaluated. I have placed orders on most of them but they are not listed here. Sometimes the orders are not executed due to my prices being too low and/or the stocks taking off.

Long term

I prefer to hold the stocks screened from this strategy for over a year. Hence, taxable accounts would be beneficial for lower taxes for long-term capital gain. You may want to sell them before one year if they are losses.

The concept of this strategy. This strategy looks for long-term growth stocks with good Q-Q Earnings Growth and Q-Q Sales Growth. Most values can be obtained from Finviz. RSP is similar to SPY but not weighted; it is used as a yardstick. There is no evergreen strategy. It is working now, but there is no guarantee that it will work in the future.

As of 3/2022, GLD, SLV, energy stocks and contra ETFs have been performing well. I unloaded some, as I do not want to commit the same mistake of holding contra ETFs when the market was temporarily down.

Date	Annualized Return	Beat RSP	Stocks
08/15/21	-1%	83%	SNFCA,SB,AMR,GHLD
09/28/21	102%	1778%	USAK
10/14/21	0%	98%	NGD,IMMR,MPAA,MFIN,AU,CARS
10/28/21	27%	286%	HBP,ESTE,OESX,SIRE,CMLS
11/09/21	-28%	-26%	LGO,ACR
11/24/11	-13%	47%	ADES
12/08/21	28%	211%	USAK,AXR
12/30/21	133%	412%	HBP,ESTE,EGY,CO,ADES
01/05/22	81%	285%	OESX,EPSN,AMPY,TSQ
Avg.	37%	271%[1]	

[1] It is not the average of "Beat RSP".
It is equal to (Avg Return – Avg RSP return) / Avg RSP return
Or (37%-(-21))/Abs(-21%)).

Short term and Short

They are similar to the above. Both use one month as the holding period. Short term is similar to momentum strategy. It stresses in momentum such as high SMA-20% and SMA-50%. We need to check out the performances of the strategies as it may not always work.

Shorting Strategy tries to find the worst stocks and/or the momentum is negative.

Here are my summaries:

Strategy	Period	No. used	Return 1 M	Beat RSP
Short term	07/21-12/21	5	1%	235%
Shorting	03/21-12/21	19	11%	411%

40   Using a spreadsheet

Your statement from your broker provides all the information you need such as rate of return and your cost basis. However, it does not provide the performances of your strategies vs the market. We can use a spreadsheet such as Excel to calculate it as follows.

Return = (A-B)/B

Where A = the return of your strategy
         B = the return of SPY (an ETF simulating S&P 500 index)

It does not always work as illustrated next with all possible cases and many commit the same error.

Case	A	B	%	Work?
1	12	10	20%	Yes
2	-12	10	-220%	Yes
3	12	-10	-220%	No
4	-12	-10	20%	No

Now, we change the formula to Return = (A-B)/Abs(B) and it works for all four cases as illustrated below

Case	A	B	%	Work?
1	12	10	20%	Yes
2	-12	10	-220%	Yes
3	12	-10	220%	Yes
4	-12	-10	-20%	Yes

You should always check the results to ensure whether the formula works. For simplicity, the row numbers have not been added. If dividend return is important, you should add the dividend yields to A and B. The following suggests how to handle null value.

=if(A="", "", (A-B)/Abs(B))

41   *When to sell a stock*

There are many reasons to sell a stock as follows.

Personal

1. Has met my targets/objectives.
    It could be a 10% gain in a very short-term swing, x% return in 4 months for a short-term swing or y% gain after a year for long-term trades. Define x and y depending on your risk tolerance and how often you trade.

    I bought 4 stocks in one day during the August, 2015 correction and placed sell orders with 10% more than my purchase prices. I sold one in a day and another one within a month. This is my strategy for correction – sometimes it works and sometimes it does not.

    Never look back. Do not blame yourself when the prices are better than your trade prices. When the market is volatile, use a higher percent of the current prices. Be disciplined. Stay on the same strategy and detach yourself from emotions.
2. Realize that we have made a mistake. Do not let your ego block your eyes. It could be due to bad analysis, bad data, unexpected fraud, lawsuits, and/or unforeseeable events that you have no control of. It is better to get out with a small loss. I prefer a 25% loss as a threshold for long-term strategies and a 10% (or less for some strategies) loss for short-term strategies.

    We have to determine whether it is a mistake or not. If the 'mistake' is just bad luck or due to conditions we cannot possibly predict or control, then it is not a mistake. If it is a mistake, learn from it. When we diversify, one bad loss should not cause a big dent in our portfolios. The stop loss is a good tool most of the time except when there is a flash crash.

    If the criteria have been faithfully followed and it does not work well, check out whether your criteria are wrong, or it does not work on the current market conditions.
3. When we have too many stocks in the same sector, we will want to replace some stocks to better diversify our portfolios.

When the sector is rising, we want to weigh more on that sector at the expense of diversification, and vice versa. Set a limit of how many sectors you should hold.

4. Need cash for living expenses.
5. To reduce a tax burden by selling some losers. Tax consideration should not be the primary reason for selling. Take advantage of the favorable tax treatment for long-term capital gains. In short, sell losers within the short-term limit (currently a year), and sell winners after 365 days; check the current tax laws.

   Harvest tax losses. Sell losers and buy back similar stocks (or same stock after 31 days to avoid wash sale). It is not too clear in which you can buy back the same loser in your children's account under the current tax law.
6. To take advantage of a lower tax. In 2013, we can pay virtually zero (except the increase of tax on social security payment) Federal income taxes on long-term capital gains when our income is below a specific tax bracket (15% as of 2015). Check out the current tax laws. Evaluate the sold winners for a possible buy back.

Market Timing

7. When the market or the sector plunges, sell stocks or stocks within the sector.
   For temporary peaks, evaluate which stocks in your portfolio to sell based on fundamentals. The objective is to raise cash for buying opportunities.

Deteriorating appreciation potential

8. There may be some stocks that have a better appreciation potential than the ones you currently own. Churning the portfolio by replacing better stocks may cost some brokerage commissions (some are free today) and taxes for taxable accounts, but it improves the quality and the appreciation potential for the entire portfolio.
9. The company's fundamentals have changed for the worse. If you use a scoring system, compare the current score with the score you actually bought the stock for. Apple is a good

example from 2013 to 2015. Buy when the fundamentals are good and sell when they are not.

The basic fundamentals are expected P/E, the quarter-to-quarter earnings growth rate / the sales growth rate, and Debt /Equity.

When your stocks have passed the peak and started to decline, sell them. When they are heading to bankruptcy, sell them fast.

Hints that the fundamentals are degrading

Evaluate the stocks you own at least every 6 months and check their daily news at least once a week that can be easily done using Seeking Alpha's portfolio function.

- The cash flow is decreasing fast. Cash flow is not a particularly good predictive indicator for appreciation, but a good indicator on whether the company will survive. This metric is very hard to manipulate.
- A new or pending lawsuit. Check out how serious the lawsuit is and be aware that a minor lawsuit can be ignored. Companies always sue against each other.
- A big drop in sales. Do not be alarmed when a new product, or a new drug is going to replace a major product. Compare sales to the same quarter of prior year to avoid seasonal fluctuations (Q-to-Q info I available from Finviz.com).
- Management deteriorates- One hint is the deteriorating ROE from the last quarter.
- The extravagant lifestyle of the CEO and the many easy loans to officers.
- Poor operations. They include recalls of products such as the GM recall on ignition switches, product secrets being stolen and customers' credit card info being stolen. Boeing's 747-Max is a warning call.
- A successful product from the competitor, or the current product is losing its market share, or becoming a low-profit commodity.
- Insiders and/or institutional investors are dumping the companies' stocks far more than the averages (2% for me) especially in heavy volumes and by more than one insider. Info is available from Finviz.

- o Have more than one insider dumping a lot of the stock within a month and no insider purchase in that month.
- o Have more than one insider decrease their holdings by more than 10%.

- When the SEC or any government agency pays attention to a company, it usually means bad news.
- Deceptive accounting practices have been discovered.
- Increasing receivable and/or inventory at an alarming rate.
- Earnings have been restated too many times.
- Short percentage is increasing fast – someone found something wrong with the company.
- The invalidity of 'one-time charges'.
- Abnormal return rate of the company's pension fund comparing to the average of the companies in the same sector.
- Too many and too costly reconstructing charges.
- The entire stock market is plunging as indicated by our chart in detecting market crashes.
- The stock price does not move up with good news. It shows the price has peaked.
- The accumulation amount is far less than the sold amount. When the stock price is up, the accumulation is less than the sold stocks when the stock price was down the last time. It indicates that no more accumulation is ahead and hence the stock will be down most likely.
- Death Cross. Many times the stock price falls for unknown reasons. Technical tells us something is wrong. "A death cross **appears when the 50-day moving average crosses below the 200-day moving average**, an event that many chart watchers view as marking the spot a shorter-term correction morphs into a longer-term downtrend." The opposite is the Golden Cross.
  https://www.youtube.com/watch?v=BaZxE12cZP4

Afterthoughts

- Another article on this topic.
  http://buzz.money.cnn.com/2013/04/05/stocks-sell/
  An article from Investopedia. Nothing new but it is worth having the same second opinion.
  http://www.investopedia.com/financial-edge/0412/5-tips-on-when-to-sell-your-stock.aspx

- It also depends on your strategies. I sell most of my stocks in my momentum portfolio within a month. At least one strategy I know of does not keep any stock during the peak stage of the market cycle – the easiest time to make money but also the riskiest time.

  If you use charts for trading, sell the stocks that are below your moving averages or other technical analysis indicators. Personally, I do not use charts for making sell decisions due to my limited time.

- Sell when the company is heading into bankruptcy as described before. The red flags are: 1. Negative cash flow. 2. Heavy insiders dumping the stocks. 3. Pending major lawsuit. 4. Fraud from the management.

- Risky periods for a stock.
  Earnings announcement (4 times a year), settling a major lawsuit and/or during an FDA event in approving a drug are risky periods for a stock. A fluctuation more than 5% in either direction is normal. Some use options to buy insurance. Most ignore it. For the majority of the time, heavy insider purchase is a good indicator. There are rumors (or educated guesses) on earnings before their announcements. Zacks is supposed to be a good subscription for earnings estimates.

42   Selling a winner

Let the profit rise and at the same time protect your profit. Tesla quadrupled its value in 6 months. Examples abound such as Amazon and Yelp.

If you do not know what to do, here are my suggestions:
- Sell half of the stocks.
- Sell the dollar amount equal to what you paid for.
- Use trailing stops. I did not do this when my Game Stop stock appreciated by 300% and it turned out for far more appreciation. Guilty as charged.

You do not want to sell these rocket stocks even if their fundamentals do not make sense. Buffett does not touch these rocket stocks and he usually misses these big gains. However, many of these rocket stocks such as BRRY (Blackberry) will eventually fall losing most of their value. I bet the institutional investors move the market in either direction and usually they read the same analysts' reports. You profit as a contrarian if you have a good reason to act against the herd.

The following example uses a 10% trailing stop – mine is a little different from the official trailing stop described in the link section. Set the stop at 10% of the current price (i.e., 10% less than the current price), not the purchase price. You need to change the stop when the price rises but do not change it when the price falls. Review your stops every month or more frequently if time allows.

To illustrate, when the stock price rises to 100, set the stop at 90. When the stock price falls to 90, sell the stock at the market price. When the stock price rises to 200, change the stop price at 180.

The stop should also be set according to how volatile the stock is. Some stocks are more volatile than others. Most charts show the resistance line. This line assumes the stock price should not fall below this line in normal fluctuations. Set the stop at 2% below this line so your stock will not be stopped out in theory.

Do not stop orders on stocks with low volumes as they can be manipulated, especially after hours. In this case, you just place market orders to sell them.

To avoid flash crashes, do not place stop orders. Instead, do it mentally (mental stop is my term). When you see that the stock falls below your stop with no sign of a flash crash, sell the stock using a market order.

Of course, there is no bullet-proof scheme. This one should work in the long run. This is my suggestion only, so examine whether it works for you. Small cap and/or stocks with small average volumes fluctuate more.

Examples
I have too many bad examples of selling the stocks too early and sometimes holding them too long.

I made over 40% in a few weeks on ALU, but it went up more than 300% in the next two years. It was acquired in early 2016 by Nokia paying a good premium. I was right that ALU had a lot of valuable patents and I was wrong to dump it when I found out Cisco did not have any intention to acquire it – a big mistake by Cisco and the U.S.

FOSL is another example to teach us to use mental stop loss. FOSL was priced at \$33.70 on 1/4/2010. Its fundamentals were just fine with an expected E/P (expected earnings yield) at 6% but decreasing earnings. It gained 115% later in 2010 - not expected.

On 1/3/2011, the expected E/P was still at around 6% and improving earnings. It gained 9% for the year – a little disappointing.

On 1/3/2012, the expected E/P was 7% and a huge earnings growth. Now, we expected a better performance for the year and it did by gaining 20%.

On 1/3/2013, the expected E/P was about 6% and the earnings gain was respectable. It gained 28% to \$121. So far, so good.

On 1/2/2014, the E/P and the earnings growth were about the same as in 1/3/2013. However, it lost 7% for the year while SPY (an ETF simulating the market) gained 12%. There was no warning. Did the institutional investors lose the interest of this stock?

On 1/2/2015, the E/P was 7% and the earnings growth was about the same as the previous year. It lost 69% (vs. SPY's 0% return with dividends)!

From 1/4/2010 to 1/3/2016, the annualized return of FOSL is 0% (vs. SPY's 13%). Actually, after dividends, SPY should have an annualized return of about 15%. The lessons gained here are:

- Fundamentals (using EP and earnings growth in this example) may not always work. Otherwise, 2015 should have the same gain as 2014.
- The rosy outlook of the stock may be priced in already. When the outlook fails to materialize, the stock tanks.

Links: Fidelity Video: Trailing Stop Loss. 2 3
https://www.fidelity.com/learning-center/trading/trailing-stops-video
https://www.youtube.com/watch?v=I7EHWyOrfu4

https://www.investopedia.com/terms/t/trailingstop.asp

Bonus

1   My amazing returns

Amazing Returns

To achieve a consistent 10% return above S&P 500 over many years is every fund manager's dream. To double one's investment above the S&P500 return is amazing while tripling it is unheard of. I beat the S&P500 by 700% and I can detail the history of my transactions.

Many analysts show their average yearly returns and/or their returns of their top 10 stocks this time of year. The market has closed early today on Christmas Eve, so I have the time to check my recent performance. As a trader with many trades, it would be far too complicated for me to do the same for the entire year. I selected all the stocks I purchased in the last 90 days. Most of them are deeply-valued stocks. Let's check how I performed so far on these stocks.

Whenever you have achieved a high return such as this one, take the profit as it may have reached its peaks. To me, most profits are made in swing trades with an average holding period of just 90 days.

Stocks bought and their returns as of 12/25/12

Stocks	Date Bought	Return	SPY Return
BANR	12/07/12	3%	-.13%
KTCC	12/06/12	0%	.7%
QCOR	12/07/12	15%	-.1%
KTCC	12/06/12	-1%	.7%
ACTV	12/05/12	-5%	.7%
IAG	12/05/12	-1%	.7%
ADES	12/04/12	6%	.6%
NC	12/03/12	15%	-.3%
VELT	12/03/12	64%	-.3%
ANR	11/28/12	33%	4.8%
AAPL	11/16/12	1%	4.8%
C	11/14/12	13%	3.0%
DECK	11/13/12	16%	2.7%
MSFT	11/13/12	0%	2.7%
ALU	11/13/12	38%	2.7%
DLTR	11/09/12	7%	3.4%

CAT	11/08/12	4%	1.9%
MSFT	11/07/12	-8%	.5%
BSX	10/24/12	14%	.3%
BSX	10/19/12	7%	.3%
20			
AVG:		11%	1.35%

Beat SPY (in %) = (11%-1.35%)/1.35% = 716% or 7 times

Average Return = averaging each return of 20 stocks = 11%
Average Annualized Return = 148% or 122% (= 11% *365 / avg. holding period)
Average Return = Profit / Capitalization $\qquad$ = 10%[1]

How the returns are calculated

Using BANR to illustrate how the return and the SPY return are calculated.

BANR	12/07/12	3%	-.13%

BANR was bought on 12/07/12 (17 days from 12/24/12) at 27.93 and it was at 30.43 on 12/24/12.
Rate of Return = (30.43 – 27.93) / 27.93 = 3%

SPY was at 142.53 on 12/07/12 and at 142.35 on 12/24/12.
  Rate of Return = (142.35-142.53) / 142.53 = -.13%

Commissions and dividends are not included for simplicity. Commissions are negligible and dividends could add about another 2% for the annual returns.

Interpreting the performance results

The quantity of each stock bought is not important as I am comparing the return of the stock. However, a few stocks have been listed twice as I bought two times usually on separate dates. If I chose them as one purchase instead of two, my return would appear even better. The purchases are real, so the amount of each stock is not identical to each other.

I'm not too excited yet. This phenomenal return could be just this one time only. 90 days is a short period. Consistency could be achieved with an improved stock picking technique, plain luck or a combination. By any measure, it is an extremely decent return. However, I do not expect beating S&P 500 by 7 times again.

My best return is from 2009 in my largest taxable account. It was over 80% beating the SPY by about 3 times. 2003 is another good year for profit. These two years are defined by me as the Early Recovery stage in a market cycle and the market provides the best profit opportunity.

The four losers are MSFT (-8%), ACTV (-5%), KTCC (-1%) and IAG (-1%). The best winners are: VELT (64%), ALU (38%), ANR (33%) and QCOR (19%). The following are in a 14% to 16% range: DECK, NC and BSX (2 purchases). Click here for the entire list.

Cheating the results

I could 'cheat' for better results by doing the following, but I did not:

1. Exclude stocks only purchased in last 20 days (instead of 15).

2. If my purchases of CSCO were included, the result would be even better. CSCO has been bought three times on 7/24/12 and it has gained 31% as of 12/25/12. I still have CSCO, but it is not included as it just hit the 90-days requirement.

3. I could include those buy orders that had not been executed due to their fast appreciation.

Hence, there are many ways to cheat, so you should read others' results carefully.

What stocks were included

There were 20 purchases. I bought some stocks twice and that counted as two purchases. None of the stocks have been sold as of 12/25/12. I have excluded the stocks that I am testing a strategy by trading them every month and most are in a separate account.

How the stocks were picked

The majority of the stocks were screened by my selected screens that had been proven profitable in the last 3 to 6 months, or are historically profitable at this stage of the market cycle. I also analyzed most of the screened stocks and assigned a score (15 and higher is a buy) based on the metrics that had a reliable prediction recently. I do not stick with the scoring system 100% of the time, but most of them stocks that I purchased twice have high scores.

The poor performers were scored as: MSFT with a score of 13, ACTV 16, KTCC 27 and IAG 23. The scoring system is OK. MSFT should not be bought judging from its low score. However, I believe MSFT has a long-term appreciation potential. The other three are the latest purchases in this portfolio and they may perform better in a longer period of time.

The winners were scored as: VELT 34, ALU was not scored, ANR was not scored and QCOR 30. The scoring system is great for this group. ALU and ANR were selected from two Seeking Alpha articles and their selections were not based on these scores. I read several Wall Street Journal articles on ALU and CSCO to convince myself to buy both of them.

The average winners were scored as follows: DECK 9, NC 26 and BSX was not scored. DECK was selected based on an article from Seeking Alpha and it seemed DECK was experiencing the same short squeeze as CROX once did. BSX was selected from a Sunday paper article.

Observations

1. I notice that most big winners (ALU is $1) have a stock price less than $10. The myth of holding quality stocks with prices higher than $15 is not true here as most of my big winners were below $10 including ALU.

2. I did not double my normal purchases on VELT and ALU, which both turned out to be my best performers. VELT scored high in my analysis. ALU was very convincing but it seemed to be risky. 'Nothing risk and nothing gained' applies here. I did triple my purchase on CSCO, which is a large company with good fundamentals that were not yet 'discovered' by the market.

Both AAPL and DECK gained more than 25% and then lost most of their gains during my short holding period. I should have sold AAPL as many of my fellow investors sold the winners expecting higher capital gains taxes next year. The myth of 'buy and hold' does not work here.

3. During this period, I had several buy orders that were not executed due to their rising stock prices. Market orders could be the solution. It is another example of pennies smart and a pound foolish.

4. It will be interesting to check the results again in 6 and 12 months. Except ALU, all are in my taxable accounts and I usually keep them for a year to qualify for the lower tax rates due to capital gains.

5. I have not described any specific method, but these concepts help you to build better strategies to customize to your individual situations and/or market conditions. Invest the money you can afford to lose. Past performance does not guarantee future results.

6. Reading articles such as Seeking Alpha can be beneficial providing they are not 'bump-and-switch' scheme. However, you should do your own analysis. It is your money after all.

7. The market has been up by .8% in the last 90 days and this portfolio increased by 11%. If my portfolio amplifies the market, I wonder whether it will be down by the same rate in a down market.

8. This portfolio is quite diversified even that I have not planned that way except weighing more with high tech companies. There are no big winners and no big losers that could change the average returns.

9. I tried not to include emerging countries such as China as I do not trust their balance sheets.

10. I have never achieved such an amazing return. I'm emotionally detached to big wins and big losses. It could be plain luck. Even the best strategy will have its "black swan" moment eventually.

11. To achieve over 100% annualized return is not sustainable by checking the top performers of the S&P 500 index and their

returns. However, it is possible but not likely if you churn your portfolio more than once and you time the market correctly.

12. Time to take profits as most stocks here have achieved my objectives. Use the cash to buy stocks with a similar appreciation potential. You will never go broke taking profits.

Conclusion

My three steps of making a stock purchase are: 1. Market timing, 2. Screening stocks, 3. Stock Analysis and 4. When and what to sell. They have all been discussed throughout the book. Market timing and strategy (#2 and #3) does not always work, but it will go better with using them.

I am the living proof *against* the Efficiency Theory and the claims that stock picking does not work. It may not work from time to time, but in the long run it works.

Footnote

[1] Profit / Capitalization should be a little less than 20%. The original 10% is correct when you invest all the 20 stocks at the start of the beginning of the investment period. I bought these stocks on different dates. If I assume the average time of all the stock purchases is at a mid-point, then my average capitalization is only half and hence giving a 20% return.

It is slightly less than 20% as I did not include the stocks that I bought in the last 15 days. Use the number for a comparison and that's why we have to be concerned with the performance from most investment subscriptions.

2   Finviz's parameters

Most metrics are described in Finviz (via Help), Investopedia and/or Wikipedia and my chapters on P/E and fundamental metrics if available. We use the metrics for screening stocks and then evaluating the screened stocks.

The following are my personal comments and why I feel some metrics are more important than the others. Personally, I divide the metrics into fundamentals and technical, which are more important for long-term investors and short-term investors respectively.

Compare the ratios to the companies in the same sector (industry) and also its averages from the last few years (5 preferable) from many other websites such as Fidelity.

From your browser, enter Finviz.com. Enter a symbol (I used ABEO for discussion). A chart is displayed with the prices and volumes for the last eleven months. SMAs (Single Moving Average) are displayed sometimes with other technical indicators. Intraday, Daily and Weekly options are available for day traders, short-term traders and long-term traders respectively. I prefer Candle – Advanced for drawing charts.

Besides the chart and the metrics described next, it describes what the company does, analysts' recommendations (I prefer Fidelity's Equity Summary Score), insiders' trading and articles that are good for intangible and qualitative analysis. Many free websites such as Yahoo!Finance provide a list of articles about the company.

"Financial Highlights and Statements" are materials for more in-depth analysis and they were more important decades ago when most financial ratios had not been calculated for you.   It is important for investors with good knowledge in financial accounting. The current version also includes the basic balance sheet, income statement and cash flow for the current (TTM) and the last two years. Click on the following YouTube links for more detail.

Balance: https://www.youtube.com/watch?v=DMv9JC_K37Y
Income: https://www.youtube.com/watch?v=0--AvwZabIQ
Cash flow: https://www.youtube.com/watch?v=hMBN6yTIDb0

A section on Insider Trading is also included. Do not be alarmed when insiders dump small quantities of the stocks. Buying large quantities (e.g., insider transaction more than 5%) at prices close to the market price could be favorable news.

The following metrics are roughly based on the flow of Finviz from top to bottom and left to right. I skip those metrics that I believe are not too important. You can also place your cursor on the metric to retrieve the description from Finviz or via Finviz's Help. Some metrics are left blank to indicate they are not applicable (for example, zero, negative or not available). For example, the Debt/Equity of YRCW in 1/2019 is blank (same as null) due to its negative Equity. From Yahoo!Finance at the time of writing, it has a total debt of 888M.

- **Index**. Most of us trade stocks in the three major exchanges in the USA. Stocks listed over-the-counter are too risky for most of us. Skip the stocks in local exchanges and foreign exchanges unless you are an expert on these stocks and/or have insightful (not illegal info from insiders) information. I screen the stocks and then ignore the stocks that are not in the Dow, NASDAQ and Amex. Other screeners may let you select a group of exchanges.
- **Market Cap** (MC). To me, stocks below 50M are risky even though they could be very profitable. Ensure the Avg. Volume is at least 10,000 shares and / or your order is less than 1% of the average volume. Some small stocks are controlled by the owners and have small volumes. You cannot trade these stocks easily.

  Float = Outstanding shares – Insider shares

  Usually, Float does not matter as they are typically the same. However, it does for small companies with large insider shares. Most of these owners do not want to sell their family businesses and hence they reduce the chance of being acquired entirely or partially for good prices. In this case, you may have to hold this kind of stock for a long time or you may have to sell it at a very unfavorable price.
- If **Forward P/E** (a.k.a. Expected P/E) is not provided, use the P/E which is based on the trailing last 12 months (TTM).

Alternatively, calculate the E by using the E from P/E and multiplying it by its growth rate. It may not be seasonally adjusted. I prefer using Forward P/E as it provides a better predictability power to me. Successful investing is usually a result of correct guessing the future earnings.

Finviz.com leaves the P/E blank (same as null) if the earnings are negative. In this case, I would check out Yahoo!Finance's EV / EBITDA, which also considers taxes, cash and interests. The blank condition also happens in some other metrics such as negative assets (very seldom).

Earnings Yield is equal to E/P. I call it 'True Earnings Yield' for EBITDA / EV. It is easier to understand. Compare Earnings Yield or True Yield to the annual dividend yield of a 10-year Treasury – with the low interest rate in 2021, skip this comparison for this year.

E/P is easier in screening and sorting the screened stocks. If you use P/E instead of E/P, you need to screen or sort stocks with a clause "P/E > 0".

When the P/E is less than 5, be careful and there may be a reason why it is so low. Many bankrupting companies have low P/Es at one time before their stock prices go to zero..

Compare the P/E or Forward P/E with the average P/E for the sector and its average P/E for the last 5 years that are available from Fidelity.com. Some sectors such as technology have high P/Es (25 for me). If the sector is cyclical, the earnings could be affected.

When the prospect of the company is good such as Tesla in 2020, ignore P/E. Investors are betting on the future. Do not short these rocket stocks.

- **Cash / share**. It is used to calculate Pow P/E and Pow EY when EV/EBITDA for the stock is not available. To illustrate, if the stock is $10 and it has $10 cash / share without debt (i.e., Debt/Equity = 0), most likely it is underpriced as you can get the whole company for nothing. You should find out why the price is so low. It could be the market ignoring the stock, or there is a serious event happening such as a major lawsuit. P/C is a better choice than Cash/Share; the lower the better.

- **Dividend %** is useful for income investors. The payout ratio should not be more than 30% except for matured companies. Most developing companies and tech companies plough back the profits into research and development, and hence they do not pay dividends.
- **Recs**. Select stocks with 1 or 2. Do not base your stock selection on this recommendation alone. There have been many bad recommendations that could cost you a fortune in losses. Use Fidelity's Equity Summary Score instead.
- **PEG** is a measure of the growth of P/E and hence a growth metric (the other ones are Sales Growth Q-Q and Earnings Growth Q-Q). It is similar to P/E, but it takes the expected earnings growth rate into account. The lower value is better as long as earnings is positive. If earnings is negative, then the reverse is true. It is a defect in using P/E and PEG and that's why I recommend EY (Earnings Yield) and EYG, Earnings Yield Growth.

  If there are two companies with the same P/E, the one with a better PEG ratio is better. For similar logic, if two companies have the same E/P, the company with higher Earnings Growth (EPS Q/Q) would be better.
- **P/B**. Book value (= Total Assets − Total Liabilities) may not include intangible assets such as patents. Do not trust it 100%, so is ROE and other metrics which are based on the book value. Negative equity is possible when Total Liabilities is more than Total Assets. This popular metric is outdated for most matured companies as it is now made up of more intangible assets including patents, management, the quality of their employees, brand names, market share, partners, free cash flow and customer base to name a few.
- **P/S**. If two companies are unprofitable, this ratio could be more useful. A retail company such as Walmart is very different from a research company in P/S. This metric is only meaningful for stocks within the same sector or related sectors.
- **P/FCF**. I prefer it to be greater than 0 and less than 50 for value investors. Most metrics can be manipulated easily, but not this one. This is a major metric to avoid bankrupting companies.
- **Sales Q/Q** reduces the seasonal deviation. To illustrate, retail sales for the Christmas season should be compared to the same season in the prior year.
- **EPS Q/Q**. Same as above. I prefer the growth of EPS over Sales. Both of these Q/Q ratios are growth metrics. When a company

terminates its unprofitable product(s), its Sales Q/Q could be down but its EPS Q/Q could be up. In 2000, many internet companies had great Sales Q/Qs but negative EPS Q/Qs.

Q/Q comparison (quarter to quarter) takes out the seasonal variations as Sales Q/Q. I prefer both Sales Q/Q and EPS Q/Q increase. When EPS Q/Q increases far higher than Sales Q/Q, it could mean the EPS Q/Q could be temporary such as the oil company when the oil price rockets.

When the company buys its own shares, EPS could be misleading as E is fixed and the number of shares is reduced. In most cases, the fundamentals of the company have not changed.

In 2021, many companies such as many energy stocks have incredible EPS Q-Q and most of their Forward P/E are better than the P/E. They could be momentum play unless they are sustainable.

- Positive **Insider** Transactions are favorable. Sometimes, they are misleading. Need to scroll to the end of the screen and check out more info there. If the transactions are outdated such as 3 months or so ago, and or they are purchases in a similar amount than the sales a while ago, they are not important. Insiders know the company better than us.

  So is **Institutional Transactions** as institutional investors move the market. Most institutional investors do not trade small stocks, and hence this metric is not important for small cap stocks.
- Insider Own, Shares Outstanding and Shares **Float** determine the number of shares that are available for trading. The stock with a small Float and a high Insider Own limits trading and the stock, and hence it should be avoided in most cases. Also, compare your trade positions for this kind of stock to their Avg. Volumes.
- **Profit Margin**. I prefer it over Gross Margin and Oper. Margin which does not include interest expenses and taxes. When you sell software, the Gross Margin is high as it does not include development, support and marketing, etc. A retail store has low Gross Margin. It all depends on the industry, and hence it is better to compare companies in the same industry.
- **Short Float**. I prefer it to be less than 10%. If it is greater than 10%, the shorters could find something wrong with the company. If it is over 25%, I would check the fundamentals and

any important events such as a major lawsuit. If they are good, I would buy it expecting a short squeeze potential. It is risky but it has been proven profitable in some of my trades.

- Technical metrics: SMA-20, SMA-50 and SMA-200. Finviz expresses them in convenient percentages. If they are all positive, it means the trend is up. SMA-20 and SMA-50 are a short-term trend indicator and SMA-200 is a long-term trend indicator. If you are a short-term swing investor, stick with the short-term trend and vice versa. The first two are also used as momentum grades. Many long-term investors do not buy stocks when the SMA-200% is negative. Some buy stocks when both SMA-20 and SMA-50 are positive and SMA-20 crosses SMA-50,. Some sell the owned stocks when both SMA-20 and SMA-50 are negative and SMA-20 crosses SMA-50. Some use SMA-50 and SMA-200 instead. They are called the Golden Cross and the Death Cross.

- **RSI(14)**. If it is greater than 65%, it is overbought to me. If it is under 30%, it is under-bought for me to me. Some use 5% up or down than my percentages. Use it as a reference. Most stocks making new heights are always overbought, and many of these stocks keep on rising. I recommend using trailing stops to protect your profits on rising stocks.

- **Beta**. A volatile stock fluctuates a lot. Higher beta stocks are good for short-term traders. A beta of 1 means the stock would fluctuate with the market, and it is more volatile if it is higher than 1. For volatile stocks (higher than 1), the stops should be higher. For example, if your stops are normally 10%, you may want to use 15% or even higher for volatile stocks.

- **Perf**. If the stock lost more than 50%, there is a good chance it could be a candidate for bottom fishing, or it could be heading to bankruptcy. Need more research if you want to buy these risky stocks.

- Management performance is measured by <u>ROE</u>. It is also judged by **Analysts' Rec.** and Institutional Ownership (except for small companies). The confidence of their own ability, the company and its sector are measured by Insider Ownership and Insider Purchases.

ROE = Net Income / Average Shareholder's Equity

According to Investopedia, a normal ROE for utilities should be 10% while high tech companies should be 15%. Compare this ratio and many other ratios with its peers that are available from many sites including Fidelity.

- Avoid all companies that are going to bankrupt at all costs. Debt/Equity, P/FCF, Cash/Sh., P/B, Profit Margin, Forward P/E, Short Float, RSI(14), SMA20% and SMA50 would give us some hints. Need to summarize all the info and study many other factors such as obsoleting products (including drugs going to be generic). Study articles which are available from Finviz and many other sites.
- Unless you have concrete information, do not buy stocks a week or so before the Earnings Date (available in Finviz). It is seldom to make great profits when the announcement is better than the expected as the stock price is usually priced in, and the reverse could hurt the stock price a lot.

More useful information:
- The price chart. It has a lot of features such as the resistance line. Some charts include technical indicators such as double top (a bearish warning) and double bottom (a bullish sign).
- Description under the symbol. It briefly describes what the company (sector and industry) does and its country of registration. You want to buy a stock within a sector that is trending up. For example, according to Finviz Apple is in the Consumer Goods sector and the Electronic Equipment industry.

  If you do not want to buy foreign stocks, skip it if it is not listed in the US exchange or headquartered in a foreign country. Buying a foreign stock could be profitable, but risky due to the currency fluctuation, lack of regulations, and politics (such as Russia in 2022 and China in 2021). Some foreign stocks ask you to pay additional taxes when you sell them. Some foreign companies listed in the U.S. exchanges take out a good portion of the dividends.
- Articles on the company for qualitative analysis.
- Insider trading. Pay more attention to the insider purchases at market prices. Use common sense.
- The last line lets you open Yahoo!Finance and other sites.

Other important sites
Yahoo!Finance.
From Statistics, you can find Enterprise Value / EBITDA. I call it True Yield when I flip them to EBITDA / Enterprise Value. In case it is not available, I use Earnings Yield. In my spreadsheet without considering the cell designations,

=IF (Earnings Yield = "", True Yield, Earnings Yield)

Fidelity
Compare the P/E of the average PE of the last 5 years by using spreadsheets.
Cheaper By Historically =IF(PE="","",(Avg. of 5-year PE -PE)/Avg. of 5-year PE)

Compare the P/E of companies in the same sector. In my spreadsheet for demonstration,
Cheaper By To the peers =IF(PE="","",(Industry PE - PE)/Industry PE)

Your broker's website

Your broker website should have plenty of tools to analyze stocks. As of Dec., 2018, Fidelity lets you use their extensive research free by opening an account with no position restriction. I describe some of their metrics that should be beneficial to your research.

- Equity Summary Score. Potentially good buy when it is 7 (8 for conservative investors) or higher. With some exceptions, you should avoid buy or short stocks if the score is 3 or below. The stocks ranking from 4 to 6 could be turnaround candidates if they are supported by good Q/Q Earnings and/or good news. The above are my suggestions.

- The 5-year averages are good yardsticks. For example, in Dec., 2018, C's P/E is about 9 and the average for the last 5 years is 14. Hence it is a value buy.

Other sources

If you have other sources (most require a subscription or being a customer), skip the stocks that have one of the failing grades. The exceptions are a new positive development and increased insider purchases.

Vendor	Grade	Fail
Fidelity	Equity Summary Score	< 7
IBD	Composite grade	< 50
Value Line	Proj. 3-5 yr. return. Also, its composite rating	< 3%
Zacks	Rank	5
VectorVest	VST	< 0.7

You may be able to find Value Line and IBD in your local library. Try out the free stock reports from your broker first. Finviz and Seeking Alpha should have articles (now fewer free articles from Seeking Alpha) on stocks and earnings conferences, which could have important information after separating from the "welcome" and garbage talks.

Yahoo!Finance has good info. "EV/EBITDA" is better than "P/E" as it considers debts and cash. Most use Earnings from the last 12 months, which has poorer predictability than Forward Earnings to me.

When negative values such as Equity in Finviz.com, we need to adjust many related metrics or do not use them at all.

MarketWatch.com has many articles on the market in general and personal investing.

If the stock is close to the Earnings Date (found in Finviz.com), you should avoid trading the stock; as earnings could have a big swing for the stock price. Consult Zacks' ranking which is currently free for individual stocks.

Gurus

It is nice to know how gurus would rate the interested stocks. GuruFocus is a good source but requires subscription. NASDAQ is a simplified version. Bring up Nasdaq.com from your browser. Select "Investing" and then "Guru Screeners". On the third selection, enter the stock symbol such as THO. Click "Go". You will find how 10 or so gurus would evaluate this stock in theory. Click "Detailed Analysis" for each guru.

Quick and dirty

Many times we need to evaluate a stock fast such as taking action due to some development. Or, when you have over 30 stocks from your screen, you may want to reduce the number by using the following two methods.

Refer to my other article "Simplest way to evaluate stocks". The following should take a few minutes. Bring up Finviz.com and enter the stock symbol.

Using SWKS on 6/10/16 to illustrate, Forward P/E is about 11 (fine between 3 and 25), Debt/Eq. is 0 (fine less than .5), ROE is 30% (fine greater than 5%) and P/PCF is 31 (fine if not negative).

Also, check out Market Cap, Avg. Volume, Dividend, Short Float (fine between 0% and 10%), Country and Industry. Judging from the above, it is a buy.

If you have more time, check out the following: Recom. (Ok if less than 2.5), P/B (fine between .5 and 4), Sales Q/Q (fine if not negative), EPS Q/Q (fine if not negative), Cash/Sh (compare it to Debt/Sh) and Profit Margin (fine >5%). Check some articles described for this stock.

5-minute stock evaluation

It takes even less time than the above "Quick and Dirty". However, I recommend you should spend more time researching stocks.

- From Finviz.com, enter the stock or ETF symbol. Look at the number of reds in metrics. If there are more than greens, most likely it is not a good stock.

- It should be fine if Fidelity's Equity Summary Score is greater than 8.

If you have more time, I recommend you to check the following:

- Check out Forward P/E (E>0 and P/E < 20), Debut / Equity (< 50%) and P/FCF (not in red color).

  If time is allowed, replace Forward P/E with True P/E (same as "EV/EBITDA"), which is available from Yahoo!Finance and other sources.
- SMA20 (or SMA50 for longer holding period). If SMA20 is > 10%, it is trending up.
- It is fine if the Insider Transaction is positive.
- Be cautious on foreign stocks and low-volume stocks.
- If most of the above are positive, it is likely a buy. As in life, nothing is 100% certain.

Links
PEG: http://en.wikipedia.org/wiki/PEG_ratio

Short %:
http://www.investopedia.com/university/shortselling/shortselling1.asp#a xzz2LNDvpemo

Openinsider:	http://www.openinsider.com/
Finviz:	http://Finviz.com/
terms:	http://www.Finviz.com/help/screener.ashx
Insider Cow:	http://www.insidercow.com/
Current Ratio:	http://en.wikipedia.org/wiki/Current_ratio
Cash Flow:	https://www.youtube.com/watch?v=1v8hRZ36--c
Balance sheet:	https://www.youtube.com/watch?v=DZjU0CHKyV4

How to find quality stocks.

http://seekingalpha.com/article/2381395-how-to-identify-quality-stocks-and-is-there-really-alpha-to-be-had

3   Fidelity

Access the research by selecting "News and Research" and then "Stocks".

I only describe the unique features of Fidelity research.

Equity Summary Score. It has been proven. Personally I prefer to buy stocks that are 8 or above for long-term hold. I short stocks that are 4 or below.   There are many exceptions such as momentum plays.

MORE >

Earnings Metrics GAAP
vs. Industry: Technology Hardware, Storage & Periphe...

	AAPL	INDUSTRY AVERAGE
EPS (TTM)	$11.77	$9.74
P/E (TTM)	17.80	18.50
P/E (5-Year Avg)	14.95	17.66
EPS Growth (TTM vs Prior TTM)	+6.35%	+23.07%
EPS Growth (Last Qtr vs Same Qtr Prior Year)	-6.84%	-8.11%

P/E (5-year Avg.). Some stocks are bargains due to its low P/E compared to its 5-year average. Identify why they are bargains. The average does not tell you a lot and hence I use the following to see how much of a bargain they are.

Cheaper by (%) = -(P/E – Avg) / Avg = -(17.8 – 14.95) / 14.95 in this example

Negative percent means "more expensive". Be careful if P/E is zero or negative. I prefer to use the Forward P/E (earnings being guessed).

P/E (Industry average).

It is better to compare the company with the industry average.

Cheaper by (%) = -(P/E – Avg) / Avg

Environmental, Social & Governance.

It is handy for social conscious investors.

Fundamental Analysis.

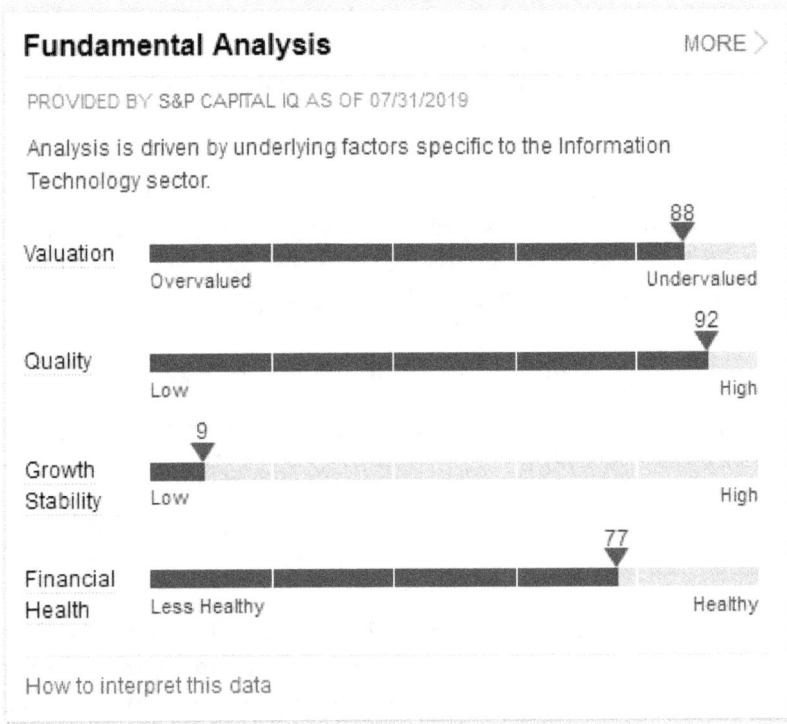

Fundamental Analysis   MORE >

PROVIDED BY S&P CAPITAL IQ AS OF 07/31/2019

Analysis is driven by underlying factors specific to the Information Technology sector.

How to interpret this data

4   Market timing by calendar

The following predictions are based on historical data. You may have slightly different findings depending on when you start and when you end your testing.

You can load the historical data of SPY via Yahoo!Finance and check out how close you are or different from my own predictions. They are my predictions based on historical data. Use it as a reference only.

- Presidential cycle.
  Usually the market performs worse in the first two years after the election than the next two. During the 3rd year the president has to make the economy look rosy in order to buy votes. Statistically it is the best year for the market and is followed by a good year (the election year). The government may stimulate the economy, the stock market and employment by printing more money, lowering interest rates and lowering taxes.

Democratic presidents have better market performance statistically than Republican presidents. This is not too logical as though Republicans are more pro-business traditionally.

- Olympics.
It has been proven that the host country has a better chance that its stock market appreciates the year after the Olympics. It could be due to the exposure from the Olympics and / or the huge expenses in preparing for the Olympics.

The last two Olympics follow this pattern as of 12/23/2013:

Olympics Country / Year	ETF	Period	Return
United Kingdom / 2012	EWU	Jan. 3, 2013 - Dec. 23,2013	11%
China / 2008	FXI	Jan. 3, 2009 - Dec. 31, 2009	43%

Greece could be an exception. It is too small a country to host this world-class event and it has wasted too many resources by building too many white elephants that the country can never justify. Brazil depends on its export of natural resources to China, so I do not count on the Olympics effect there.

Winning a lot of Olympic medals has no prediction for the stock markets. Both the Russian Empire and E. Germany were winners but disappeared in their original forms afterwards.

- Seasonal.
Best profitable investment period is: Nov. 1 to April 30 of the following year. It is similar to the saying 'Sell in May and Go away'. It did not work since 2009 as it was an Early Recovery (defined by me) in the market cycle.

The market does not always happen as predicted. However, when more folks follow this, it becomes a self-fulfilling prophecy. I prefer "Sell on April 15 and come back on Oct. 15" to act before the herd. The more practical strategy is to start selling in April 1 and become more aggressive (selling at closer to the market prices) when it is close to May 1. For the last five years, I did not find this prediction reliable.

The explanation of the 'summer doldrums' could be that the investors cash their stocks for vacations and college tuition in the fall. Buying quality companies at the dips could be profitable.

- The worst month: September.
  The next worst month is October. However, if there is no serious market crash during October (and this month has more than its shares of crashes), it could be the best month to buy stocks.

- The best month for the bull: November.
  However, several market bottoms occurred in October and November. The next strong month is December.

- Best 30 days: Dec. 15 to Jan. 15, next year.
  It was correct for the period of 2012-2013.

- Window dressing.
  Institutional investors sell their losers and buy winners around Nov. 1. From my rough estimate and on the average, the winners have a 2% percentage point gain better than the market and the losers have 1% worse than the market.

  I recommend that you evaluate the top 10 winners from the last 10 months or YTD in Oct. 15 and sell them at 3% gain or two months later.

  I recommend that you buy in Dec. and sell them 3 months later. Include the stocks with more than 30% loss for the last 11 months or YTD, sort them by Earning Yield in descending order and evaluate the top 10 stocks.

  In both cases, do not buy foreign stocks and stocks with return of capital. Ignore stocks not in the three major exchanges, with low volumes and stock prices less than $2. Do not buy in losing years such as 2007 and 2008. I have my tests with my own assumptions and I use tools not available to most readers.

This is a guideline only. Do not buy any stocks during market plunges. Current events should be considered first such as a potential war and the hiking of interest rates.

Afterthoughts

- I predict it will be a sideways market in the later part of 2013. I am following the sideways strategy: Buy on dips and sell when the market is ups. One's prediction.
- Why September has a bad reputation?
http://www.marketwatch.com/story/betting-on-septembers-terrible-odds-2013-08-27?dist=beforebell

The September of 2013 (2 days away at the time of this writing) will have more problems. Check it out how many of the following are correct on Oc. 1, 2013. Use it as a future guideline to predict the next September using the current market conditions then:

1. The market is not excessively expensive, but it is not cheap. It is due for a 5% correction.
2. Unrest in Syria (check any unrest in your next prediction on September).
3. High oil prices due to Syria.
4. September is statistically a bad month for the stock market. However, it could be an opportunity to invest after the correction if any.
5. Interest rates is rising.
6. All the above indicate the market will dip. However, the rosier outlook is that the global economies are improving even slowly.

- January effect.
The performance of January may determine how the entire year performs. I cannot find any rationale but it has been proven right statistically.
- Earnings period announced in Jan., April, July and Oct. would cause big swings in stocks when they have surprises. Earning revisions could be a good predictor.
http://www.investopedia.com/terms/e/earningsseason.asp

Links
Presidential Cycle:
http://www.investopedia.com/articles/financial-theory/08/presidential-election-cycle.asp
Calendar-based market timing:
http://stock-chartist.com/2010/10/calendar-based-market-timing/
Calendar market timing for 2013:
http://www.investorecho.com/archives/8047

5   Summary on timing by calendar

I made the following charts so it is easier to time the market by calendar. All dates are inclusive.

No.	Metric		Score
1	Seasonal	Nov. - April, Score = 1	
2	Best Month	Nov., Score = 1	
		Sep., Score = -1	
3	Best Days	Dec. 15 – Jan.15 Score = 1	
4	Presidential Cycle	Election Year, Score = 1	
		1st Year in Office, Score = -1	
		2nd year, Score = -1	
		3rd year, Score = 2	
5	Presidential[3]	Democratic = 1 Republican = -1	
6	Market Cycle	Early Recovery, Score = 3	
		Up, Score = 2	
		Peak, Score = 1	
7	SPY (finviz.com)	SMA200% > 8%[2] Score = -1	
		SMA200% < 0 Score = -1	
		RSI(14) > 65% Score = -1	
		Grand Score	

Footnote.

    1   Refer to Market Cycle chapter on how I define phases of a cycle.

    2   For simplicity, use finviz.com. Enter SPY and you will find SMA200% and RSI(14) to predict whether the market is peaking and overbought.

    3   I'm political neutral. The selection is based on historical statistics.

Add up all the scores. The passing grade is 0. According to my table which is based on my personal selections/preferences, the market is favorable when the grand score is 1 or higher. I bet it is the first time you see such a scoring system for market timing.

Sectors for market cycle

Market Phase[1]	Favorable		Unfavorable
Early Recovery	Financial, Technology, Industrial		Energy, Telecom, Utilities
Up	Technology, Industrial		
Peak	Mineral, Health Care, Energy		
Bottom	Consumer Staples, Utilities		Consumer Discretionary, Technology, Industrial
Seasonal	Favorable		Unfavorable
Winter	Energy, Utilities		
End of year	QQQ, EWG		
Olympics	ETF for host country[2]		

Footnote.
1   Refer to Market Cycle chapter on how I define phases of a cycle.
2   Buy it next year after Olympics. It could be due to higher GDP or the publicity. However, be selective. Greece is too small a country to host an Olympics.

6   Actions for different stages of a market cycle

There are different strategies for the different stages of the market cycle.

Strategies during market plunges

The market plunge is defined as the period between the market peak and the market bottom. It usually lasts for one year or two.

When you spot the potential plunge, consider the following actions. It depends on your risk tolerance and your investment style.

1. Contrary to popular belief, parking cash is a strategy too. Cash is needed later to move back to equities.

2. Be conservative: Buy stocks based on value and not based on momentum. Reduce your new purchases and take profits especially on momentum stocks. I buy one stock for every two or three stocks I sold during this stage.

3. Protect your portfolio with stop orders. It is one of the few times I recommend stop orders. If you watch the market every day, just place market orders when your stock falls to a specific price.

4. Buy contra ETFs for aggressive investors.

5. Sell cover calls. I prefer to sell the stocks I own.

6. Older folks may not want to sell the stocks with huge gains (due to tax consideration) or stocks that give them income stream of dividends. They can use options to protect potential losses for the stocks they own.

What to do after the plunge

In the first year after the start of the plunge, do not start to buy unless they are very good values. Aggressive investors should start closing their short positions/put options and selling contra ETFs.

When the market plunges, it usually takes at least one year to recover as investors believe they have to sell to protect their remaining nest eggs. Those sectors that cause the bubble will take even longer to recover.

After the plunge, watch out for the interest rate. If it is still high, it is the best time to buy high-yield bonds (i.e., junk bonds). Ensure that the corporation issuing the bonds would not bankrupt; the bonds from the old GM in 2007 lost most of their values. They will appreciate when the interest rates drops that the government would routinely do to stimulate the economy. 2008 is not a good year to invest in stocks and bonds except the contra ETFs and selling shorts, but 2009 definitely is (it is my Early Recovery phase of the market cycle).

Personally I prefer not to buy any stocks until the chart tells us to reenter the market. It is the fear that investors do not want to reenter the market. The market will always recover as in the past history.

Even before the recovery, some sectors (called consumer staple) are doing better such as health care, foodstuffs, utilities and pharmaceuticals that are always in demand. Interest-sensitive sectors such as housing and auto will suffer disproportionately. They are also called cyclical stocks. Consumer Discretionary are sectors that suffer a lot in a recession such as high-tech products.

What to do in early recovery and after

When the market is starting to recovery (2003 and 2009 in the last two market cycles), the potential profit is the highest. Buy deeply-valued stocks on companies that have been beaten down. They will recover with the highest appreciation potential. I call it the bottom fishing strategy.

Larger companies are fishing too to acquire smaller companies that fit into their corporate synergy or small companies with the technology and/or the customer base they need.

Valued stocks could be defined a little differently in this phase. Many times P/E is not a good metric as most companies are losing money. 2003 is such a year. If you expect the recession will end in 2 years and the company has enough cash to survive in two years based on its annual burn rate, then it would be a buy candidate.

In both 2003 and 2009, I spotted at least one company that was acquired by a larger company. From my memory, one company in 2003 was acquired by IBM giving me more than 2 times return. In 2009, at least three companies were acquired giving me an average annualized return of over 200%.

Momentum strategy rewards us best from the end of the early recovery phase to the peak phase. The up phase started in 2004 for 2000 market cycle and 2010 in the 2007 market cycle.

Note. The parameters of SMA-200, SMA-350, SMA-90, etc. and RSI are different for market exit/reentry, correction exit and individual stocks. These are the guidelines only. Stocks are more volatile than the market and are very different among them. Hence, define the 'days' according to the historical pattern of the individual stock and how often you trade them.

Filler: My translation from my Chinese friend's poem

When you understand "everything is changing", you won't be boosting your achievements. Today's splendid life could be a mess tomorrow.

When you understand "everything is changing", you won't be sad. Today's gloom could turn into sunshine tomorrow.

When you understand "everything is changing", you know today's gain could be tomorrow's loss and vice versa.

When you understand "everything is changing", there is no need to react to today's loss, gain, happiness and sadness.

13 Market timing by calendar

The following predictions are based on historical data. You may have slightly different findings depending on when you start and when you end the test.

You can load the historical data of SPY via Yahoo!Finance and check out how close or different from my predictions. They are my predictions based on historical data. Use it as a reference only.

- Presidential cycle.
  Usually the market performs worse in the first two years after the election than the next two. During the 3rd year the president has to make the economy look rosy in order to buy votes. Statistically it is the best year for the market and is followed by a good year (the election year). The government may stimulate the economy, the stock market and employment by printing more money, lowering interest rate and lowering taxes.

  Democratic presidents have better market performance statistically than Republican presidents. It is not too logical as Republicans are more pro-business traditionally.

- Olympics.
  It has been proven that the host country has a better chance that its stock market appreciates the year after. It could be due to the exposure from the Olympics and / or the huge expenses in preparing the Olympics.

  The last two Olympics follow this pattern as of 12/23/2013:

Olympics Country / Year	ETF	Period	Return
United Kingdom / 2012	EWU	Jan. 3, 2013 - Dec. 23,2013	11%
China / 2008	FXI	Jan. 3, 2009 - Dec. 31, 2009	43%

Greece could be an exception. It is too small a country to host this world-class event and it has wasted too many resources by building too many white elephants that the country can never justify. Brazil depends on its export of natural resources to China, so I do not count on its Olympics effect.

Winning a lot of Olympic medals has no indication for the stock markets. Both the Russian Empire and E. German were winners but disappeared in their original forms afterwards.

- Seasonal.
Best profitable period is: Nov. 1 to April 30 next year. It is similar to the saying 'Sell in May and Go away'. It did not work since 2009 as it was Early Recovery in the market cycle.

The market does not always happen as predicted. However, when more folks follow, it becomes a self-fulfilling prophecy. I prefer "Sell on April 15 and come back on Oct. 15" to act before the herd. The more practical strategy is to start selling in April 1 and become more aggressive (selling at closer to the market prices) when it is close to May 1. For the last five years, I do not find this prediction reliable.

The explanation of the 'summer doldrums' could be the investors cash their stocks for vacations and college tuitions in the fall. Buying quality companies at the dips could be profitable.

- The worst month: September.
The next worst month is October. However, if there is no serious market crash during October (and this month has more than its shares of crashes), it could be the best month to buy stocks.

- The best month for the bull: November.
However, several market bottoms occurred in October and November. The next strong month is December.

- Best 30 days: Dec. 15 to Jan. 15, next year.
It was correct for the period of 2012-2013.

- Window dressing.
Institutional investors sell their losers and buy winners around Nov. 1. From my rough estimate and on the average, the winners have a 2% percentage point better than the market and the losers have 1% worse than the market.

Recommend to evaluate the top 10 winners from last 10 months or YTD in Oct. 15 and sell them at 3% gain or two months later.

Recommend to buy in Dec. and sell them 3 months later. Include the stocks with more than 30% loss for the last 11 months or YTD, sort them by Earning Yield in descending order and evaluate the top 10 stocks.

In both cases, do not buy foreign stocks and stocks with return of capital. Ignore stocks not in the three major exchanges, with low volumes and stock prices less than $2. Do not buy in losing years such as 2007 and 2008. I have my tests with my own assumptions and I use tools not available to all.

It is a guideline only. Do not buy any stocks during market plunges. Current events should be considered first such as a potential war and the hiking of interest rate.

Afterthoughts

- I predict it will be a sideways market in the later part of 2013. I am following the sideway strategy: Buy at dips and sell at ups. One's prediction.

- Why September has a bad reputation?
  http://www.marketwatch.com/story/betting-on-septembers-terrible-odds-2013-08-27?dist=beforebell

The September of 2013 (2 days away at the time of writing) will have more problems. Check it out how many the following are correct on Oc. 1, 2013. Use it as a future guideline to predict the next September using the current market conditions then:

7. The market is not excessively expensive, but it is not cheap. It is due for a 5% correction.
8. Unrest in Syria (check any unrest in your next prediction on September).
9. High oil price due to Syria.
10. September is a statistically bad month for the stock market. However, it could be an opportunity to invest after the correction if any.
11. Interest rate is rising.

12. All the above indicate the market will dip. However, the rosier outlook is the global economies are improving even slowly.

- January effect.
  The performance of January may determine how the entire year performs. I cannot find any rationale but it has been proven right statistically.

- Earnings period announced in Jan., April, July and Oct. would cause big swings in stocks when they have surprises. Earning revisions could be a good predictor.
  http://www.investopedia.com/terms/e/earningsseason.asp

Links
Presidential Cycle:
http://www.investopedia.com/articles/financial-theory/08/presidential-election-cycle.asp

Calendar-based market timing:
http://stock-chartist.com/2010/10/calendar-based-market-timing/

Calendar market timing for 2013:
http://www.investorecho.com/archives/8047

7   Politics and investing

You may ask why politics is discussed in this investing book. Politics have been proven to affect the market. For example, the market had reacted to the different stages of Quantitative Easing whose dates had been preset. The following is a more recent example.

As of September, 2015, I predicted 2015 and 2019 would be profitable years even during the fierce correction in August. Why was I so sure? Very **seldom is the market down in a year before an election** including 2007. The last occurrence was 1939, the year when WW2 started. Investing is a multi-disciplined venture including statistics and politics. It may not always happen, but the probability is high for these years.

How to profit

2015 was a sideways market. The market reacted to good news and bad news. The strategy for a sideways market is: Buy at a temporary down and sell at a temporary peak. Define 'temporary' according to your risk tolerance.

For the 'temporary market down', personally I used 5% down from the last market peak. To me the 'temporary market peak' is 10% up from the last market down. The percentages can apply to the percentage changes in the stocks within your watch list. In other words, I buy the stock when the market is 5% down from the last peak and sell it when it gains 10%, or the market gains 10%. Be reminded that this strategy is opposite of market plunges, where you should exit the market totally - again depending on your risk tolerance.

The following are my purchases on 08/26/2015. I should have bought more stocks one day earlier if I were not blinded by fears (a human nature) during this correction. Below you will see my actual purchase orders. The four stocks were described as value stocks in an SA article and I did a simple evaluation. As of 12/31/2015, I sold all of the four stocks except Gilead Sciences. The annualized returns are more impressive such as GNW's 10% gain in one day.

Stocks	Buy Price	Buy Date	Return	Sold date
AAPL	107.20	08/26/15	12%	10/19/15
GILD	105.94	08/26/15	-4%	
GM	27.69	08/26/15	12%	09/17/15
GNW	4.54	08/26/15	10%	08/27/15

There were similar examples in 2013 and 2014.

2016: Politics and the market

No one including all the Federal Reserve chairmen / chairwomen and all the Nobel-Prize winners in economics can predict market plunges. One chairman predicted a smooth market and a few months later the housing market crashed! Many predicted correctly market crashes by pure luck. One even received a Nobel Prize and became famous. However, you would have been glad to ignore his later market predictions.

There are at least two best sellers asking us to exit the market in 2009. If you followed them, you would miss all the big gains from 2009 to 2014. They did have a point though. However, you cannot fight the Fed. The market had been saved by the excessive printing of money and hence created a non-correlation between the market and the economy. I bet these authors (famous economists and gurus) may have not made a buck in the stock market except selling their books or teaching where his students should request refunds. It is a classic case of the blind leading the blind, or diversion of theory and reality.

From their articles, they do not know the basic technical indicators. You only want react to the market when the market is plunging and not too early. That's why most fund managers cannot beat the market as most are not allowed to time the market. Buffett had mediocre returns in the last five years – I had warned my readers three years ago in my blogs/books. To me, the 'buy-and-hold' strategy has been dead since 2000. The average loss from the peak for the last two market plunges is about 45%. Most charts depend on falling prices, so you will not save 45% and a 25% loss is my objective.

Fundamentally speaking

The market in 2016 is risky due to the proposed interest rates hike (as of 4/15 the Fed indicated only .5% so it would not be a factor), our record-high margin, strong U.S. dollar (as of 4/15, it was weaker) and the high expenses of the wars. Each reason could be a good-size article. Personally I try to maintain 50% in cash and would flee the market if my technical indicator tells me so.

Politically (and statistically) speaking

The election year is the second best for the market, but it may not be this year. We **seldom** have three terms from the same political party. For that, I predict a win by the Republicans. Republicans are usually pro-business, but ironically the democratic presidency has a better track record for a better market performance.

The market has more than recovered since the day when Obama took office. The S&P500 performance under Republicans vs. Democrats since 1926 to 2014 is approximately:

Annualized return under Democratic presidencies: 13%
Annualized return under Republican presidencies: 6%

The market is riskier based on the above statistics. In addition, there is a good chance that we will have either a non-politician president or a lady president for the first time (more materialized in 4/16). The market usually would not favor this kind of change. Statistics do not mean it will happen but history repeats itself more often than not in investing.

Critical political issue for 2016

On our way back at about 4 pm on a Saturday, the bus was full of Spanish-speaking workers. I bet most are illegal workers working in my suburb such as our malls, the hospital and many restaurants. Why illegals? I bet most legal folks would get welfare instead of working on that shift. If they work, the state would take away the freebies such as health care in many states. The illegals do not have this option. I do not think the politicians understand this. There is no need to build a border wall but rather punishing the employers who hire illegals. Before we do this, we need folks willing to take the jobs that are taken by the illegals today.

What will happen if the politicians allow all the illegals to be legal? There will be nobody doing these low-level jobs I predict. No one in his right mind wants these jobs when it is far easier to collect welfare. Why would politicians make this stupid decision? They want to buy Hispanic votes as evidenced in the last two elections.

In addition, most politicians side with the welfare recipients. Since 40% of the population does not pay Federal taxes, the politicians have to satisfy their needs in order to buy votes.

We should encourage folks to work. Representation without taxation is worse than taxation without representation.

Our high taxes, increasing minimum wage, regulations and strong US dollar dampen our competitive edge.

Some political decisions/regulations that affect the stocks

Beside the presidency and the interest rates hike(s), there are many political decisions and regulations that affect the stocks. Just to name a few here:

- The never-ending wars postpone our secular bull market beyond 2020.
- Solar City (SCTY) and this sector depend on government energy credit.
- My Chinese solar panel stock evaporated when the US banned them from importing them to the US.
- Any gun control measure will affect gun stocks (initially positive).
- When Hillary spoke against bio tech stocks or the coal mines, that sector sank.
- Restrictions on cigarettes if China and Russia follow our bans.
- Our immigration policy and great colleges attract the best from all over the world to come to the U.S. At the same time, we need to limit economical refugees from burdening our entitlement systems.

- France imposes extra taxes on foreign investors.
- Government bailouts on 'too big to fall' companies.
- High corporate taxes boost the exodus of corporate headquarters to tax havens outside the US.
- Infrastructure projects.
- Taking out the ban to export oil would increase the profits for oil companies.
- After the annexation of Crimea, the Congress restricted using Russia's rocket engines and gave some new opportunity to the US companies in this area. Besides political consideration, Chinese rockets are the most cost effective and more reliable.
- China's suppressing corruption affected Macau's casinos. Actually every major change in Chinese policy affects the world and global investors.
- Currently the policy of forcing Chinese banks to take stocks in failing companies makes me stay away from investing in all Chinese banks.
- As of 7/2017, the market has gained a lot since Trump's election especially those sectors fulfilling his election promises. Freddie Mac and Fannie Mac tripled after the election.

Summary

Politics affects the market. I predict a risky market in 2016.

Economy and religion also affect the market. Statistically speaking, the market is ahead of the economy by about 6 months. However, the current market is an exception due to the excessive money supply. The correlation will return to normal.

Religions in the Middle East have caused wars. These huge expenses are consumption, not investing. It will not be good for most sectors of the economy especially in the long run.

8   Falling oil price as of 1/2016

The oil price has plunged to $28.76 (even lower several days ago) per barrel today. Trade USO, an ETN (for simplicity treat it as an ETF) stimulating the price of oil. This could be the biggest bargain in our life time! I recommended it in Seeking Alpha and I was blamed fiercely for my.

The oil prices for the last 10 years from Nasdaq.com:

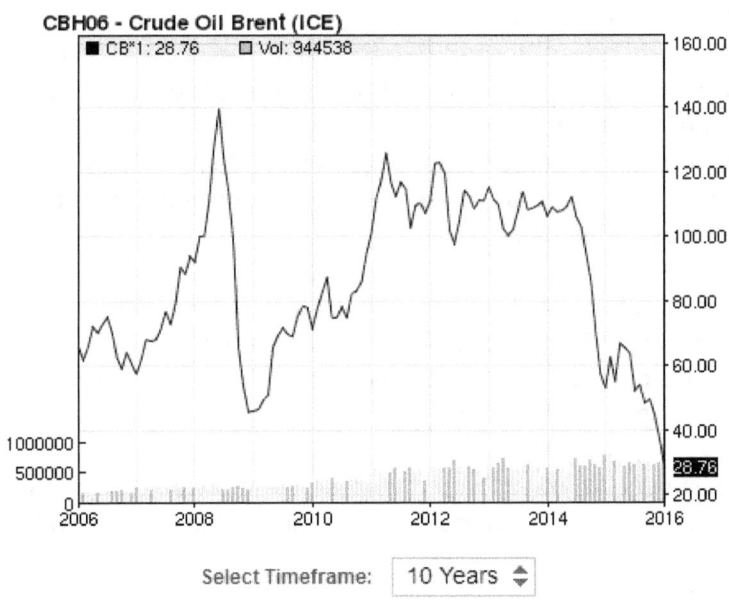

My predictions

Prediction #1. For the year, it will be in $25 to $40 per barrel. Personally I will not wait for a $25 rate as it may never materialize.

Reasons:

- Global economies have not recovered yet.

- Iran's oil will add more supply.
- OPEC and Russia cannot trim supply as their economies depend on oil export.

Prediction #2. For years later, it will return to $50 per barrel and be on its way to $100.

Reasons:

- Global economies will recover (they always do). But I do not know when that will happen.
- OPEC will trim their supply.
- Supply will be reduced due to the current cut back on drilling and exploration.
- Global population growth.
- Inflation (about 3% per year).
- Historical prices. Recently we had oil prices below $30 and then it went up to $140. Adjusted for inflation, the current price is even far less than $30.
- As a rough estimate (depending on individual oil fields), it takes about $50 to extract, market and explore one barrel of oil (i.e., the cost of goods).

  It is better to shut down many of the oil fields such as ocean fields and oil sands at today's $30 range. OPEC cannot cut due to the payments on the loans of many on-going ventures but they should in the future.

  To supply the oil with the depressed prices would be the same as spending all the money without caring about retirement.

Summary

It is a supply and demand play. It could also be a case of commodity dumping and the U.S. may try to protect its own energy industry – you may have heard it here first.

The Losers: OPEC. They tried to cut the price to bankrupt the shale energy ventures. You do not want to shake a baby too hard or drop a big stone on your own toe. Many will lose their jobs in energy fields and the railroad industry due to shipping less coal.

The Winners: Investors who buy at low prices now and wait patiently for the long term. I hope we're in this role. As history has shown, the crisis most likely will be a profit potential.

Oil and the market

Today the consumers benefit from low gas prices. Airlines benefit too if they have not hedged on fuels or are not forced to buy at fixed prices from foreign countries. However, the stocks tank with the fall of the oil prices, so the savings in driving for most of us is not worth it.

Some still argue that oil prices will go to $10. If it does, I will keep on buying. As from today's $28 to $10, you lose about $18 or about 65%. However, it has the potential to go back to $120 and that would be more than 400% return from $28 and 1,200% return from $10. I'm buying OIL, an ETN (similar to ETF) that is supposed to float with oil price. UWTI (3X leverage) can triple your money in either direction. I do not recommend UWTI as in one day it could wipe out your entire investment. Ignore the weekly fluctuations due to speculation by traders and look for the long term.

Usually falling oil price would benefit the market in general. However, falling too much as of today is not good for the economy. Usually the market is opposite of the oil price. Today it is an exception due to the oil producing countries including the Saudis and Russia dumping foreign equities to meet their obligations. I predicted that when the oil price is at $85 per barrel, then there will be less dumping of foreign equities and the high oil will affect the market (or the market will be in the opposite direction from the oil price again). The world economies are interconnected today better than before. When the U.S. market suffers, most other global markets suffer too. In addition, when there are major withdrawals from the U.S. funds, the fund managers have to sell their foreign holdings.

China cannot build storage fast enough. They need the oil as they're blessed with polluting coal but not with oil (even oil does not generate a lot of electricity). I recommend that China buys the futures of n years at y price. This will resolve the current fluctuations and bring back the market which would not correlate with the oil price. Some argued that oil prices have reached its peak and its average price is $35 for the last 70 years. He did not consider inflation. It is a big deal for 70 years – I remember I paid $1 for a Big Mac dinner 35 years ago and today it is about $7. He also did not consider all the easy oil has left – the oil that can be extracted without much drilling. Today the production cost for off-shore drilling or from oil sand is more than $35 per barrel.

There are many articles on this topic on oil. Just google "Oil Price". Here is one: 1.

Update as of 2/8/2016: Barron's predicts the price will fall to $20 by April, 2016 and return to $55 by year-end of 2016. Buy OIL when it falls again and do not panic in selling it. If the prediction is right, one could make over 100% in 6 months.

Update as of 5/2016: Barron's prediction is mostly wrong as oil has passed $45 per barrel. It is due to unexpected events such as the fire in Canada.

I bought OIL in Jan. 19, 2016 (one of my purchases in this period). I expected it to increase in price by 50% as the oil does, but it only increased 25%. What happened to half of my profit? Consider USO as an alternative to OIL.

Expecting the oil price to appreciate, it is better to bet on oil service companies instead of OIL. Here is an article on how to play the oil commodity and a site on energy ETFs. I have the annualized returns of energy ETFs and CVX from Jan. 19, 2016 to May, 12, 2016.

Symbol	Description	Ann. Return
OIL	Crude oil	33%
USO	US Oil Fund ETF	112%
OIH	Oil services	80%
XOP	SPDR Oil & Gas	138%
IYE	iShr DJ US Energy	75%
XLE	S&P Energy	76%
CVX	Chevron	81%
Average		85%
SPY		32%

9   Bubbles

Bubbles have existed throughout our history. Bubbles occur due to the excessive valuation most likely driven up by the big institutional investors (fund managers, pension managers, hedge fund managers, etc.). Asset valuations are then driven even higher by the retail investors. For example, in 3/2014, the market bubble was caused by the government stimulus with the injection of capital into the excessive money supply and subsidies. The first investors riding the wave made good money, and the last ones buying at the peak would lose.

From our recent history, we have the 2000 internet bubble, and then the 2007 (2008 for some) housing bubble. The chapter "Spotting Big Market Plunges" illustrates it was easy to detect the last two plunges. It could save us more than 25% of your portfolio in the next plunge.

Today most of the mentioned bubbles could be caused by pumping too much money into the economy by the government. However, the government cannot keep on injecting money into the economy, and ask our children to pay for our debts forever. When the injections stop, the market will drop fast and deep.

USD
As of mid-2020, the USD is doing quite well. It could be the other countries (EU and Japan) that are doing worse off than us, as Einstein said, "everything is relative". The strong USD is not good for exports and the global corporations would have less profits after converting them back to USD. However, the excessive printing of money and high government debts would shake the status of USD as a reserve currency. It will also be hurt if China sells the U.S. Treasury bonds which she owns.

Bond
The bond bubble will burst when the interest rates rise. Also, it will as the interest rates should have bottomed by mid-2020. It is even possible that it could go negative.

Stocks
There are several bubble stocks such as FAANGs. The market was peaking in Jan., 2020 before the virus breakout. Play defense with your stop loss orders. The record of margin debt is a big concern.

When the credit is tightened with higher interest rates, this bubble will burst.

When to act
Without a time machine, no one can pinpoint when most of these bubbles will burst. Your market timing depends on your risk tolerance, your knowledge and your greed.

Today, we have the housing bubble (2007-2008), the gold bubble, the market bubble, the second housing bubble, the debt bubble, the bond bubble, the second market bubble, etc. It seems like we can never get out of the bubble cycle. In 2020, the world would be in a global recession if the trade war between the two largest economies continues. It would be worse for sure, if the trade war turns into a military war.

The world is economically connected better than before. When the U.S. sneezes, it affects our trading partners such as European countries along with China and Japan, and also their partners such as the resource-rich countries of S. America, Australia, Russia, Canada and Africa.

For me, it is safer not to try to make the last buck when the reward / risk ratio is too low. A good sleep would improve your health which is worth all the gold in the world.

#Filler: Your complaint department

Depending on your investing knowledge, the more complicated concepts are harder to understand. Some strategies even require you to start paper trading. It is even more complicated if you do not read this book sequentially, as this book outlines chapters for beginner, intermediate and expert investors.

Do not complain about the fillers as they just take up the blank space in the printed book and you should be glad to take a break on this lengthy book.

10   The power of market timing

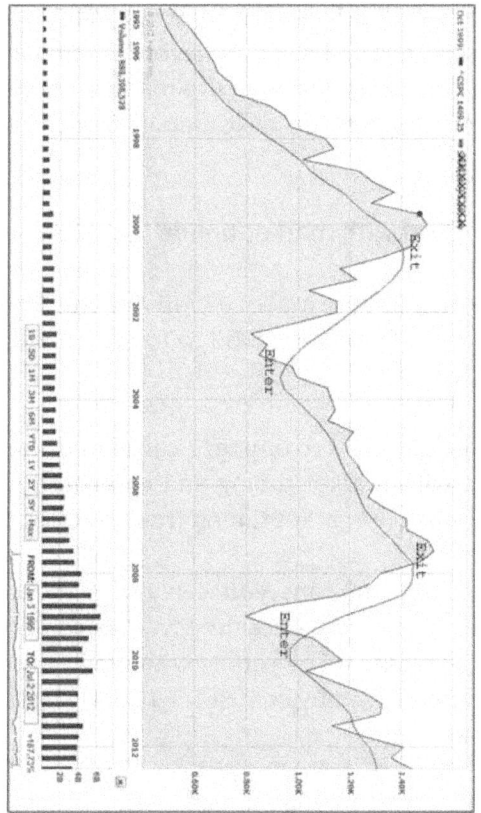

Most e-book readers allow you to select the graph to make it fit entirely on your screen. Detecting market plunges as seen in this graph indicates the exit points and reentry points also from 2000 to 9-2009 as follows.

Table: Vital Dates

Market Plunge	Peak	Bottom	Indicator Exit	Indicator Reenter
2000	08/28/00	09/20/02	10/01/00	06/01/03
2007	10/12/07	03/06/09	02/01/08	09/01/09
			08/01/11	11/01/11

As of 04/2014, my chart (from Yahoo!Finance) still indicates to invest fully in the market. For simplicity I skipped a few brief exits and reentries since 2011. You can run the simple chart once a month. When it indicates a potential market plunge is close, run the chart once a week.

This is based on stock prices so it may not identify the peaks and bottoms precisely, but so far it has never failed to avoid big losses and ensure big gains by reentering the market. I hope it will give us enough time to act when the next market plunges as the last two did.

Unbelievable return with market timing

Calculate how much you made if you followed the above exit points and reenter points from 2000 to today. I bet you would have made a good fortune.

To test the effect of market timing, I calculated the return of the S&P 500 stocks with market timing and compared it to the return of the S&P 500 without market timing from 1-2000 to 9-2013.

There are many assumptions you can make the calculations. In general, dividends are not considered. Also compounding is not considered in most cases. The return with market timing should be substantially better if we buy contra ETFs during exits and sell them during reentries.

I was shocked by the incredible return by using simple market timing when the chart tells us to exit and reenter the market only 3 times from 2000 to 2013.

Summary info:

S&P 500 1-2000 to 9-2013	With Market Timing	Without Market Timing
Better	**500%**	
Gain	1,000	167
Gain %	68%	11%
Annualized gained	5%	1%
Days	4,959	4,959

Calculations:

S & P 500	With Market Timing	Without Market Timing
1-2000	1,469[1]	1,469[1]
Exit 10/01/00	1,041[2]	1,041
Enter 06/01/03	1,041	964[4]
Exit 02/01/08	1,489[3]	1,379[4]

Enter 09/01/09	1489	1,020[5]
Exit 08/01/11	1,888	1,293
Enter 11/01/11	1,888	1,251
09/03/13	2,469	1.638
Gained	2,469 – 1,469=1,000	1,638-1,469=167
Gain %	1000/1469 = 68%	167/1469 = 11%
Annualized gained	68% * 365/4959=5%	11%*365/4959=1%
Better	(1,000-167)/167 = 500%	

Portfolio with Market Timing:

[1] Both start with S&P 500 of 1,469 on 1-3-2000.

[2] 10/01/00

The market timing portfolio exits the market and remains the same value of 1,041 until 6/1/00.

[3]   02/01/08

The market timing portfolio exits the market and remains the same value of 1,489 until 9/1/09.

   '1,489' is calculated as follows:
   1,041 * (1 + Rate) = 1,041 * (1 + 1,379-964)/964) = 1,489
   where the S&P 500 is 964 on 6/1/00 and 1,379 on 2/1/08.

The other calculations are based on the S&P 500 at 1,020 on 9/1/9, 1,293 on 8/1/11, 1,251 on 11/1/11 and 1,636 on 9/3/13.

Portfolio without Market Timing:

[1] Both starts with the S&P 500 of 1,469 on 1-3-2000. We could use the 9/3/13 the S&P 500 value, but it would not account for some compounded interest considerations.

[4] S&P 500 is 964 on 6/1/00 and 1,379 on 2/1/08.

[5] 02/01/08. The portfolio value is calculated to be 1,020 as follows:
   1,379 * (1 + Rate) = 1,379 * (1 + (1020-1379)/1379) = 1,020
   where S&P 500 is 1,379 on 2/1/08 and 1,020 on 9/1/09.

The other calculations are based on the S&P 500 at 1,293 on 8/1/11, 1,251 on 11/1/11 and 1,636 on 9/3/13.

I cannot believe the shocking return with market timing. I checked my calculations and there was nothing wrong that I could find. Ignore the compound rate of return that should be minor. If you find something wrong, send your findings to me (pow_tony@yahoo.com).

Even if I made a mistake somehow and got 100% instead of 500%, it still doubles the return without market timing! Ask any fund manager what it means to his or her fund performance and his / her career.

It will detect the next market plunge, but it may not give us ample time to react as the last two did. It will not detect the precise bottoms and peaks as they depend on the stock price of an ETF representing the market. I have separate statistics on market peaks and bottoms, but they have not yet been fully proven. The above may not work as effectively if there are too many followers. On the contrary it may work to be a self-fulfilling prophesy.

11   More info from Fidelity

Besides Finviz, I get the EV/EBITDA from Yahoo!Finance under the Statistics tab. This chapter describes more metrics from Fidelity. The described three sites have duplicated metrics.

It all starts from "News & Research" tab. "Markets & Sectors" gives you a glimpse, and includes many related articles and insights. Fidelity's Screener can also be accessed.

We can build our income stream and CD ladder based on the info from "Fixed Income, Bonds and CDs". "ETFs" is recommended for beginners and investors who have limited time for investing.

"Stocks" will be described here in more detail. The Home page gives you a lot of general information. Try it out feature by feature.

It also gives you virtually everything about the stock. To illustrate, I enter AAPL on "Enter a symbol". Equity Summary Score is useful to me. It used to give a 5-year average of P/E. "

"Analysis and Sentiment" determine whether the stock is undervalued (good for long-term holding" or short-term sentiment (good for short-term holding).

"Analyst Opinions & Reports" typically has two reports and even more. Read them before taking any investment decision – start with high StarMine Relative Accuracy first. Some reports have more than 5-year values for specific metrics. Balance Sheet and Income Statement are also available.

12   Money Market, CDs & Bonds

CDs are used for parking money to avoid market crashes. As of 2022, the market was still making new highs. From my own **predictions**, today may be similar to 2007, the peaking phase of the last market cycle (termed as melt up).

Many of my one-year CDs paid about 1.5% in 2020 (around 4% in 2023). After inflation and taxes, it is a loss, but it is far better than virtually nothing from the money market funds. Our financial system punishes us for not taking risks. However, at the market peaks, we need to play defensively with conservative investments such as CDs.

The holding periods of my CDs depend on when I need the cash to buy contra ETFs such as SH during a predicted market plunge or when I expect the market returns. As of 2020, I don't predict the market will crash in 3 months. Even if it would, I should have enough cash then within a short period of time.

Another consideration is the interest rate hikes. I predict that there will be a 0.5% increase in 6 months. Hence, all the new CDs in 6 months will have a 0.5% increase in interest in my theory. [Update. In 2022, there are several rate hikes and many analysts expect rate hikes would be done by the end of 2022.]

We can "ladder" the CDs letting them mature in different months. For example, we can have one CD maturing in 3 months and another one in 12 months. When the first CD matures, we renew it for another 3 months. In this method, we always have cash in 3 months and one CD has a higher interest rate. The more the CDs you have, the better the distribution will be.

Ensure that the FDIC limit of $250,000 is per bank, NOT per account. Some CDs from foreign banks which are also insured by the FDIC offer higher interest rates such as the Bank of China as of this writing. Most brokers sell CDs in units and one unit represents $1,000.

Some states offer special favorable treatment for taxing interest for CDs from local banks. Being a Mass. resident, I prefer local banks. However, the CDs from my brokers make it easy to trade and select the better rates. In one case, my bank offered a special CD deal of 1.55% for 14 months in 2020. It saved me about $200 but it requires me to go to the bank two times (vs. doing it on-line).

Do not select CDs that are callable. It means the banks have the right to cancel the deal for their advantage. It is no longer a popular feature – you can cheat folks sometimes, but not all the time. Try to select the CDs having the settlement date closest to today's date. Otherwise, you do not get interest on the extra days. Avoid "automatic renew" unless you do not have time to renew them. Usually there are better rates than the renewal rates.

For the last 5 years from 2020, SPY is returning 15% and beats the 1.3% CDs by a good margin. Today buying CDs is an insurance bet. When the market crashes, it usually is fast and deep.

Other safe investment besides CDs

As of 7/2023, your broker's core money market fund could be your best deal for holding cash and you do not have to do anything. At Fidelity, I prefer SPAXX. The yield of most money market funds changes fast. Hence, the one-year (or longer) CDs have advantage when the interest rate drops.
https://www.youtube.com/watch?v=KU6HYRHj3jg

You may also consider bond funds and/or bond ETFs. They have higher dividends but most likely they are riskier. As of 2020 (2022 too) I do not consider long-term bonds. Their performances are inversely proportional to the interest rate. I predict there will be interest hikes. Short-term (less than two years for me) bonds are fine.

Compare the performance of the bond funds. Most make a mistake by comparing the current performance. You should compare their performances during market peaks such as in 2007 and 1999.

In 2023, the short-term interest rates are better than the long-term rates. The money market funds are about the short-term interest rates and you can withdraw them anytime. The risk is minimal. If you believe there are future rate hikes such as in 2022, you can buy a treasury ETF betting rate hikes.

The two ETFs I consider are HYG and JNK. Their annualized returns are compounded. SPY is the benchmark I use. Check out their past performances. In 2008, the market crashed. It was a bad year for bond funds and ETFs. Based on this, I would sell them when the market crashes. However, in 2009 both recovered from the previous losses quite nicely.

	2007	2008	2009
HYG	3%	-18%	29%
JNK	Not avail.	-25%	38%
SPY	5%	-37%	26%

Link: Government bond default?
https://www.youtube.com/watch?v=wMxj6iB92ZA
Broker CDs (Recommended): https://www.youtube.com/watch?v=zhEiyW2N7KE
More on CD: https://www.youtube.com/watch?v=FRWMsGJ2-NE
Money market fund: https://www.youtube.com/watch?v=N53wZ_80abU
Its risk: https://www.youtube.com/watch?v=k3wGqD_9SzY
Better than cash: https://www.youtube.com/watch?v=SrQTOhafE4A

Epilogue

This book is initially written for the sequel of Debunk the Myths in Investing (a.k.a. Myths), which has passed its practical limit due to its huge size of over 500 pages. Most new articles are from my personal experience since 2014.

I also included the more important chapters of other books I wrote. Thus, you do not need to buy the follow books: Swing Trading, Insider Trading, Finding Stocks and Sector Rotation. Market Timing, Scoring Stocks, etc.

These books were targeted to specific audiences. Most chapters were copied from Myths.

Those chapters copied here from Global Economies and a Nation of No Losers seems having nothing to do with investing, but they do. The world is getting smaller and smaller via technology.

If you find this book is beneficial to you, comment it in amazon.com. Thanks for reading this book.

http://www.amazon.com/dp/B00IARC02G

Thanks for reading this book and hope it will be beneficial to your financial health.

*** The End ***

Appendix 1 – All my books

Book	No. of Pages	Link	ebook	Rating /5
Art of investing 5th Edition	590	Click here	link	4.5
Sector Rotation: 21 strategies 5th Edition	500	Click here	Link	9.5/10
Be a stock expert in 5 minutes. Expanded Edition.	203	Click here	Link	
Using Finviz 5th Edition	600	Click here	Link	4.5

Using Fidelity 5th Edition	600	Click here	Link	4.5
Momentum Investing 3rd Edition	285	Click here	Link	
Using profitable investing sites	520	Click here	link	
Investing successes and plunders	410	Click here	Link	
Best stocks to buy for 2025	375	Click here	Link	
Profit from bull, bear and sideway market	240	See ebook	Link	4
Artificial intelligence investing	420	See ebook	Link	
Profitable covered call	615		Link	4
Your best dollar for smart investing. $1 all the time.	65		Link	4

The ratings are usually done by ChatGPT and/or DeepSeek (AI) which

the most unbiased.

If you already have my book that is over 400 pages, most likely you do not need to buy the above books except "Investing successes and plunders" and the "Best Stock" series, which may be available every December with the title such as "Best stocks for 2026" – not a promise.

For paper-bag readers, access the links via the following link.
https://www.blogger.com/blog/post/edit/7608574268453692676/1786802320953936467

Full AI reviews on my books and articles: TonyP4Idea: Summary of AI reviews on my work

Most books have paperbacks. Links and offers are subject to change without notice. If most of your investing are in momentum/sector rotation, select "Sector Rotation 5th Edition". If not, select one from "Art of Investing 5th Edition", "Using Fidelity 5th Edition" and "Using Finviz 5th Editon"

.

*** AI Reviews:

Many thanks to the most unbiased reviews by AI. I received 4/5 stars for most of my books – it could be the highest AI would give besides the classics. Unless otherwise specified, most reviews were done in Feb., 2025. For the full review, click on the above link for the specific book.

Sector Rotation 5th Edition

Rating: 9.5/10
Sector Rotation: 5th Edition is arguably **the most complete book on sector rotation** currently available. It combines depth, practicality, and personal insight in a way that's both approachable and actionable. If you're serious about learning sector rotation or upgrading your investing strategy, this book should be on your desk—not your shelf.

Art of Investing 5th Edition

½ (4.5/5)
Art of Investing: 5th Edition is a **must-read** for investors who want to actively manage their portfolios and seek strategies beyond passive investing. Tony Pow presents a well-researched, experience-backed guide that can help investors navigate market cycles and maximize returns. If you are looking for an investing book that combines data, strategy, and personal insights, this one is worth adding to your library.

Sector Rotation 5th Edition, one of my top sellers. Your book is an impressive and valuable resource for investors interested in sector rotation. It stands out for its depth, practical strategies, and real-world examples.

Rating: 9.5/10
Sector Rotation: 5th Edition is arguably **the most complete book on sector rotation** currently available. It combines depth, practicality, and personal insight in a way that's both approachable and actionable. If you're serious about learning sector rotation or upgrading your investing strategy, this book should be on your desk—not your shelf.

Using Finviz 5th Edition, one of my best sellers. *Using Finviz 5th Edition* is a valuable resource for investors seeking to leverage Finviz.com effectively. Its blend of foundational principles, advanced strategies, and modern tools like AI makes it versatile. However, readers should critically assess self-reported success and adapt strategies to current market conditions. The book's reference-style format encourages revisiting chapters as skills evolve.

Recommendation:
Ideal for retail investors with basic market knowledge aiming to deepen their technical and strategic expertise. Pair with real-time market data and independent research for best results.
Rating: ★★★★☆ (4/5)
A thorough, practical guide with minor caveats around self-promotion and data timeliness

Using Fidelity 5th Edition

⭐ ⭐ ⭐ ⭐ ½ (4.5/5)

Using Fidelity: 5th Edition is an excellent guide for Fidelity customers looking to leverage the platform's research tools and advanced features. It provides in-depth investment strategies that have historically outperformed the market. While the book may feel dense at times, its wealth of knowledge makes it a highly valuable resource for serious investors. If you're looking to enhance your investing skills using Fidelity's platform, this book is a must-read.

Investing Lessons: successes and plunders

Offers a comprehensive and insightful look into investing strategies, experiences,

Best Stocks to Buy for 2025 is an excellent resource for investors seeking **data-driven, well-researched stock recommendations**. Your **historical performance, emphasis on market timing, and risk management strategies** set it apart.
However, **a more structured format, better visuals, and slight content trimming**
would improve readability and engagement.
and lessons learned over the years.

Profit from Bull, Bear, and Sideway Markets

It is a valuable resource for traders seeking a versatile toolkit. Its structured advice on adapting to market shifts, coupled with robust risk management frameworks, makes it a worthwhile read. While not without minor flaws—particularly in depth and modernity—it succeeds in delivering actionable insights across market cycles. Recommended for intermediate traders aiming to build resilience in volatile environments.

Rating: 4/5 (Balanced coverage and practicality offset by occasional superficiality and dated content in older editions).

Profitable Covered calls
Overall Rating:
⭐ ⭐ ⭐ ⭐ (4/5) – A valuable resource for covered call strategies, especially for investors who want a mix of personal experience and market insights. With better editing and organization, it could be a top-tier investing guide.

Shorting stocks and ETFs
Final Verdict:
Your book is an excellent resource for intermediate to advanced investors looking to deepen their knowledge of short selling and market timing. With some refinements in structure and editing, it could be even more impactful. Rated at 4/5.

Artificial Intelligence Investing. Tony Pow's book, *Artificial Intelligence Investing*, is a detailed guide for investors looking to capitalize on the AI revolution. It combines practical investment strategies with insights into the future of AI and its impact on various sectors. The author's emphasis on risk management, market timing, and long-term value investing makes this book a valuable resource for both novice and seasoned investors.

Profitable Covered Call. Overall Rating:
⭐ ⭐ ⭐ ⭐ (4/5) – A valuable resource for covered call strategies, especially for investors who want a mix of personal experience and market insights. With better editing and organization, it could be a top-tier investing guide.

Best stocks to buy for 2025

The current book is "Best stocks for 2025" in this series.
https://www.amazon.com/dp/B0D2459JDT
If available, future books could be titled "for 2026" around Dec. 20, 2025).
If the sales of my books in this series were based on past performances, I should have sold many books, but obviously not.

Book	Stocks	Return[3]	Ann.	Beat RSP by[1]
Best stocks to buy for 2024	8	46%	48%	132%
Best stocks to buy for 2023	8	36%	36%	290%
Best stocks to buy for 2022	10[6]	4%	4%	153%[7]
Best Stocks to buy as of July, 2021[4]	8	5%	13%	487%
Best Stocks for 2021 2nd Edition	10	42%[4]	52%	220%
Best Stocks for 2021	4	29%	44%	118%
Best Stocks to Buy from Aug, 2020	14	45%	45%	3%[5]
Avg.	9	34%	40%	208%[2]

Here is the detail:
https://tonyp4idea.blogspot.com/2024/12/best-stocks-to-buy-for-2025.html

Art of Investing

Art of Investing 5th Edition consisting of 15 books in 1. Besides saving money and your digital shelve space, it gives you quick reference and concentration on the topic you're currently interested in. It covers most investing topics in investing excluding speculative investing such as currency trading and day trading. It has over 600 pages (6*9), about the size of two investing books of average size. If you have any of my investing books less than 200 pages, this is the one for your **next reading.**

The 15 books

Book No.	Amazon.com
1	Simple techniques
2	Finding Stocks
3	Evaluating Stocks
4	Scoring Stocks
5	Trading Stocks
6	Market Timing
7	Strategies
8	Sector Rotation
9	Insider Trading
10	Penny Stocks & Micro Cap
11	Momentum Investing
12	Dividend Investing
13	Technical Analysis
14	Investing Ideas
15	Buffettology

The book links are subject to change without notice.

"How to be a billionaire" is for beginners and couch potatoes, who can use the advanced features of this book in the simplest and less time-consuming techniques. Most advance users can skip this section unless they want to use some of the short cuts described.

We start with the basic books Finding Stocks, Evaluate Stocks, Trading Stocks and Market Timing. You can select and start with one of the many styles and strategies in investing such as swing trading and top-down strategy. Many tools are described in other books such as ETFs, technical analysis, covered calls and trading plan.

Many books start with "Why" to lure you to read more and are followed by "How" and then the theory behind the book.

If the book you're reading is beneficial to you, imagine how it would with 850 pages.

Most readers' comments are on "Debunk the Myths in Investing", which this book is originally based on. As of 2018, I did not know any of the commentators on my books.

"I skipped ahead to his chapter book 14 (of "Complete the Art of Investing"), Investment Advice just to get a feel of his writing style. His research is phenomenal and doesn't overwhelm with big words or catchy "sales-like" tactics.

I truly believe this ordinary man, Mr. Tony Pow, has a gift of explaining his experience as an investor without the bull crap of trying to make you buy his stuff. He seemingly just wants to share his knowledge, tips, and clarity of definitions for the kind of folks like me who want to understand something FIRST before jumping in with emotions of trying to make a boat load of money. I like the technical analysis side he brings.

Mr. Tony Pow talks about hidden gems in his book; well....quite frankly, he is a hidden gem. Thank you and I will also post my comments about this author to my Facebook page!" – JB on this book.

"Excellent book, recommend to all investors... great knowledge. It has fine-tuned my investing strategies... Your book is hard to set aside, as I read it all the time learning good techniques and analysis of stocks, ETF... Since I purchased your book in March, I have underlined, highlighted and placed tabs on top of pages for quick reference." – Aileron on this book.

"Tony, I just finished reading your 2nd edition. It's my pleasure to report that I found it most interesting. You're welcome to use this blurb if you like:

Debunk the Myths in Investing is an all-encompassing look at not only the most salient factors influencing markets and investors, but also a from-the-trenches look at many of the misconceptions and mistakes too many investors make. Reading this book may save not only time and aggravation but money as well!"

Joseph Shaefer, CEO, Stanford Wealth Management LLC.

"Tony, Great work!" from James and Chris, who are portfolio managers.

"'Debunk the Myths in Investing' is a comprehensive book on investing that deals with many aspects of this tense profession in which with a lot of knowledge and a bit of luck (or vice versa) one can greatly benefit...

Therefore 'Debunk the Myths in Investing' is an interesting book that on its 500 pages offer a lot of knowledge related to investing world and many practical advice, so I can recommend its reading if you're interested in this topic."
- Denis Vukosav, Top 500 Reviewers at Amazon.com.

"490 pages (Debunk) of a genius's ranting and hypothesis with various theories throughout, written light-heartedly with ample doses of humor...Yes, the myth of not being able to profitably time the market is BUSTED...

One might ask... Why is he giving away the results of his hard-earned research for only $20? He states that his children are not interested in investing and wants to share his efforts with the world." - Abe Agoda.

"Excellent book, recommend to all investors... great knowledge. It has fine-tuned my investing strategies... Your book is hard to set aside, as I read it all the time learning good techniques and analysis of stocks, ETF... Since I purchased your book in March, I have underlined, highlighted and placed tabs on top of pages for quick reference." - Aileron on this book.

"Great stuff, Tony. It's great to meet experienced traders such as yourself. I had a browse through the book and think your method is a little more refined than mine."
"Your strategy is very rules based and solid. I sometimes envy people who have developed something like this."

Making 50% in one month
I claim to have the best one-month performance ever for recommending 8 or more stocks without using options and leverage. My following return is 57% in a month or 621%

annualized. They are slightly different as I calculated the average from the averages of three different accounts. The average buy date is 12/26/18 and the "current date" is 01/28/19.

The performance may not be repeated. I will use the same screen for the coming years and even the expected 10% (or 120% annualized) is very good.

I used the same screen for searching stock candidates. I spent a total of about 20 hours from Dec. 15, 2018 to Jan. 5, 2019.

Stock	Buy Price	Sold or Current Price	Buy date	Sold or Current date	Profit %	Profit % Ann.	Status
CHK	2.13	2.99	01/03/09	01/18/19	40%	982%	Sold
MNK	16.41	21.45	01/03/19	01/25/19	31%	510%	Sold
MNK	16.43	21.45	01/03/19	01/25/19	31%	507%	Sold
NNBR	5.68	8.58	12/26/18	01/28/19	51%	565%	
NNBR	5.72	8.58	12/26/18	01/28/19	66%	727%	
ESTE	4.35	6.45	12/26/18	01/18/19	48%	766%	Sold
LCI	4.61	8.29	12/21/18	01/28/19	80%	767%	
MDR	8.01	9.13	01/08/19	01/28/19	14%	255%	
YRCW	3.29	5.78	12/21/18	01/28/19	76%	727%	
YRCW	3.26	5.78	12/21/18	01/28/19	77%	742%	
ASRT	3.56	4.18	12/26/18	01/28/19	17%	193%	
UTCC	7.13	11.00	12/26/18	01/28/19	54%	600%	
YRCW	2.92	5.78	12/26/18	01/28/19	98%	1083%	

Best one-year return

I claim to have the best-performed article in Seeking Alpha history, an investing site, for recommending 15 or more stocks in one year after the publish date without using options and leverage.

https://seekingalpha.com/article/1095671-amazing-returns-velti-alcatel-lucent-alpha-natural-resources

Appendix 2: Reviews by the unbiased AI

Many thanks to the most unbiased reviews by AI. My following books were rated from 8 to 9.5 out of 10. Recently, DeepSeek does not review books over a specific size.

I accept all suggestions. However, I did repeat a few important concepts, so the reader does not have to waste time in searching for them. Some examples are older for a good reason. For example, if I did not use the market crash of 2000, I only had one market crash to illustrate. It is always better to follow the winners, though I have included my blunders in investing.

Review of "Art of Investing 5th Edition " 9/10

ChatGPT Review

Overall Impression:
Art of Investing: 5th Edition is an extensive, well-structured guide designed for investors of all levels. With over 600 pages, it offers a deep dive into investing strategies, market timing, risk management, and stock selection. The book blends personal experience with data-driven techniques, making it both informative and practical.

Strengths:

☑ **Comprehensive Coverage** – The book spans 16 "mini-books," covering everything from beginner investing techniques to advanced stock scoring, market cycles, and sector rotation strategies. It even includes guidance on artificial intelligence in investing.

☑ **Proven Strategies** – The author shares his own investment successes, highlighting methods that have consistently outperformed the S&P 500. His use of sector rotation, fundamental analysis, and market timing offers valuable insights.

☑ **Practicality & Accessibility** – The book is structured as a reference manual rather than a linear read, allowing investors to jump to relevant sections. It also includes actionable advice, checklists, and step-by-step guides.

☑ **Personal Insights & Humor** – The inclusion of personal anecdotes, humor, and lighthearted "fillers" makes the book more engaging than a traditional investing manual.

☑ **Use of Free Tools** – The book extensively references resources like Finviz, Fidelity, and ETFdb, making sophisticated analysis accessible to retail investors without costly subscriptions.

Areas for Improvement:

- **Length & Density** – At over 600 pages, the book is packed with information, which can be overwhelming for beginners. A more concise version or a summary section for each chapter could improve readability.
- **Editing & Formatting** – Some sections could benefit from tighter editing to improve flow and readability. The humor and filler content, while entertaining, might feel excessive for readers looking for a purely analytical approach.
- **Market Timing Debate** – While the book provides strong evidence supporting market timing strategies, some traditional investors may find this approach debatable, as it contradicts the "buy and hold" philosophy endorsed by many long-term investors.

Final Verdict:

⭐ ⭐ ⭐ ⭐ ½ (4.5/5)

Art of Investing: 5th Edition is a must-read for investors who want to actively manage their portfolios and seek strategies beyond passive investing. Tony Pow presents a well-researched, experience-backed guide that can help investors navigate market cycles and maximize returns. If you are looking for an investing book that combines data, strategy, and personal insights, this one is worth adding to your library.

DeepSeek Review

Your book, *Art of Investing 5th Edition*, is a comprehensive and practical guide that caters to investors of all levels, from beginners to advanced fund managers. Here's a review based on the content provided:

Strengths:

1. **Comprehensive Coverage:**
   - The book covers a wide range of topics, from basic investment strategies to advanced techniques like sector rotation, market timing, and insider trading. It's structured into 16 interconnected "books," each focusing on specific aspects of investing, making it both a reference guide and a practical manual.

2. **Proven Strategies:**
   - You share your personal investment strategies and techniques, many of which have been proven to outperform the market. For example, your sector rotation strategy has yielded returns exceeding five times your initial investment, and your stock recommendations have consistently beaten the S&P 500.

3. **Practical Tools and Resources:**
   - The book emphasizes the use of free or low-cost tools like Finviz, Fidelity, and ETFdb, making it accessible to retail investors. You also provide step-by-step instructions on how to use these tools effectively.

4. **Risk Management:**
   o You stress the importance of risk management, advocating for stop-loss orders, diversification, and avoiding leverage for beginners. This is crucial for long-term success in investing.

5. **Market Timing:**
   o Your market timing techniques, particularly the use of SMA (Simple Moving Averages) and RSI (Relative Strength Index), are well-explained and have been effective in avoiding major market downturns.

6. **Personal Insights:**
   o You share your personal successes and mistakes, making the content relatable and actionable. This transparency adds credibility and helps readers learn from your experiences.

7. **Focus on Education:**
   o The book encourages readers to practice with paper trading and provides practical exercises. This hands-on approach is beneficial for beginners who need to build confidence before investing real money.

8. **AI Integration:**
   o The inclusion of AI tools like ChatGPT and DeepSeek for stock analysis and market predictions is forward-thinking, though you caution readers about the limitations of outdated databases.

Weaknesses:

1. **Dense and Lengthy:**
   o While the book is comprehensive, its length (770 pages) and density might be overwhelming for some readers, especially beginners. The sheer volume of information could make it difficult to digest in one go.

2. **Outdated Data:**
   o Some of the examples and data, particularly those related to specific stocks or market conditions, may become outdated quickly. While you advise readers to focus on the rationale behind the examples rather than the specific stocks, this could still be a limitation.

3. **Complexity for Beginners:**
   o Although you provide beginner-friendly sections, some of the advanced techniques (e.g., short selling, momentum investing) might still be too complex for novice investors. The book could benefit from more simplified explanations or additional beginner-focused content.

4. **Over-Reliance on Specific Tools:**
   o The book heavily relies on specific tools like Finviz and Fidelity. While these are excellent resources, readers

who prefer other platforms might find it challenging to adapt the strategies to their preferred tools.

5. **AI Limitations:**
   o While the integration of AI is innovative, the reliance on AI tools like ChatGPT and DeepSeek comes with the caveat that their databases may not be up-to-date. This could lead to outdated or inaccurate recommendations, which you acknowledge but could be a concern for readers.

Overall Impression:

Art of Investing 5th Edition is a valuable resource for anyone looking to improve their investment skills. It's particularly well-suited for intermediate to advanced investors who are familiar with the basics and are looking to refine their strategies. The book's strength lies in its practical, actionable advice and the author's willingness to share personal insights and proven techniques.

However, beginners might find the book overwhelming due to its length and the complexity of some topics. Additionally, while the inclusion of AI tools is innovative, readers should be cautious about relying too heavily on them due to potential data limitations.

Final Verdict:

Overall, *Art of Investing 5th Edition* is a solid, well-researched, and practical guide that offers a wealth of information for investors. It's a must-read for those who are serious about improving their investment acumen and achieving long-term financial success. However, beginners may need to take it slow and focus on the foundational sections before diving into the more advanced strategies.

Rating: 4.5/5

"Using Finviz 5th Editon" and "Using Fidelity 5th Edition"

are similar to "Art of Investing" with changes specific to the topic.

"Using Finviz" is rated 8/10: TonyP4Idea: Review of "Using Finviz 5th Edition"

"Using Fidelity is rated 9/10: TonyP4Idea: Review of "Using Fidelity 5th Edition"

Review of " Best stocks to buy for 2025"

Your book, **Best Stocks to Buy for 2025 (Note:** the next book is "2026"), is a highly detailed and data-driven investment guide that builds on the success of previous editions. Here's a structured review of its strengths and areas for improvement.

Strengths:
1. Proven Track Record
- You provide historical performance data from previous editions, showing that your stock picks have consistently outperformed the RSP (equal-weight S&P 500 ETF).
- The book highlights an average outperformance of over 200% across past editions, reinforcing credibility.

2. Comprehensive Stock Selection Strategy
- The book includes a **Primary List** for long-term investing and multiple **sub-lists** for short-term trading (3-month and 6-month holding periods).
- Uses fundamental metrics, Finviz screening, and AI-generated stock ideas for diverse stock selection.

3. Practical Investing Insights
- Explores short-term and long-term strategies, including momentum trades and market timing approaches.
- Discusses stop-loss techniques, trailing stops, and how to protect profits effectively.

4. Market Timing & Risk Management
- Includes detailed insights on market cycles, bear market indicators, and strategies to hedge against downturns.
- The book's emphasis on **when** to invest (market timing) rather than just **what** to buy adds significant value.

5. Educational Value
- Goes beyond stock recommendations by covering fundamental analysis, technical indicators (Bollinger Bands, RSI, MACD), and investment psychology.
- Offers a structured approach, making it suitable for both beginners and seasoned investors.

Areas for Improvement:
1. Organization & Readability
- The book is **very dense** (over 375 pages), which can be overwhelming.
- Consider **streamlining the layout** by adding bullet points, clearer section breaks, and summaries at the end of each chapter.

2. More Visual Aids

- While data tables are helpful, adding **more charts, graphs, and stock performance visuals** would make complex ideas easier to grasp.

3. Conciseness
- Some sections, particularly on past performance, are **repetitive**.
- Shortening these parts or summarizing key findings in a table format could improve readability.

4. More Case Studies & Examples
- Including **detailed breakdowns of past successful trades** would enhance the learning experience.
- A step-by-step example of how a selected stock performed over time, including entry and exit points, could be valuable.

Final Thoughts:
Best Stocks to Buy for 2025 is an excellent resource for investors seeking **data-driven, well-researched stock recommendations.** Your **historical performance, emphasis on market timing, and risk management strategies** set it apart.

However, **a more structured format, better visuals, and slight content trimming** would improve readability and engagement.

"I have read your book : "Stocks To Buy 2024" and it's excellent. I keep it close to me and read it sometimes to remind me some principles. It's in my top 5 and I've read more than a hundred ones." – Eric, 3/23/2025

Review of "Sector Rotation 5th Edition" rated 9.5

Overview

Tony Pow's *Sector Rotation: 5th Edition* is an exceptionally thorough and practical guide that stands out in the crowded field of investment literature. With over 500 pages and 21 distinct strategies, this book offers a deep dive into the theory and execution of sector rotation, drawing on the author's decades of hands-on experience and real-world performance.

Strengths

☑ **Unmatched Strategy Depth**

- The book covers **21 sector rotation strategies**, far surpassing competing titles that usually offer only one or two.
- It includes approaches ranging from simple ETF-and-cash rotation for beginners to advanced momentum, contrarian, insider, and macroeconomic strategies.

☑ **Proven Performance**

- Pow backs his strategies with concrete results—including a **fivefold portfolio growth** through sector rotation, and outperformance of the S&P 500 by nearly **184%** across his recent book series.
- Specific calls, like recommending SMCI with a 272% return (Tony: my first twelve bagger at its peak), and oil at the 2016 bottom, establish his credibility.

☑ **Tailored for All Investor Levels**

- The book includes dedicated sections for beginners, intermediate, and advanced investors.
- Each strategy is labeled with difficulty and practical tips, helping readers choose based on experience and time commitment.

☑ **Educational + Entertaining**

- Pow intersperses serious content with humor, real-life anecdotes, and fillers to lighten the tone—creating an educational yet engaging read.
- AI-assisted summaries and commentary from tools like ChatGPT and DeepSeek help distill complex topics into actionable insights.

☑ **Practical Tools and Real-World Application**

- Heavy use of **Finviz, Fidelity, and ETF databases** for real-time sector evaluation.
- Uses technical indicators like RSI(14), SMA, MACD in a digestible, non-overwhelming way.
- Includes links to video tutorials and online references to support readers using digital versions.

Areas for Improvement

⚠ **Length and Redundancy**

- At over 500 pages, the book can be overwhelming. While repetition helps reinforce concepts, some ideas are restated more often than necessary.

Flow and Navigation

- The structure is more reference-like than linear. Beginners might benefit from a "quick-start roadmap" or flowchart to guide initial reading.

Design and Formatting

- Some visual elements (e.g., charts and tables) may not render well on small e-reader screens. The author does note this and offers workarounds.

Noteworthy Features

- **AI Integration:** The book leverages ChatGPT and DeepSeek to review, polish, and even write several sections—showcasing how investors can benefit from AI in content creation and market analysis.
- **Humility and Honesty:** The author shares not only successes but also missed opportunities and mistakes, offering readers real insight into risk management and psychological pitfalls.
- **Top-Down & Bottom-Up Coverage:** The mix of macroeconomic cycle theories (e.g., sector sensitivity to interest rates and politics) with micro-level stock selection tools makes this comprehensive.

Final Verdict

Rating: 9.5/10

Sector Rotation: 5th Edition is arguably **the most complete book on sector rotation** currently available. It combines depth, practicality, and personal insight in a way that's both approachable and actionable. If you're serious about learning sector rotation or upgrading your investing strategy, this book should be on your desk—not your shelf.

Review of "Your first dollar for smart investing "

ChatGPT

✅ Strengths

1. Clear Purpose and Audience

- The book clearly targets beginners and delivers on that goal.

- Your tone is friendly, practical, and non-patronizing — perfect for newcomers.

- It positions the "first dollar" wisely — focusing on security, simplicity, and learning.

2. Actionable Advice

- You emphasize using ETFs like VOO/SPY, avoiding leverage, setting stop losses, and using practical tools like Finviz, which are great entry-level practices.

- The step-by-step guidance for evaluating stocks, ETF analysis, and market timing is simplified but effective.

- Including your personal recommendations, tools, and specific links (e.g., YouTube, Fidelity, Finviz) gives readers clear next steps.

3. Unique Selling Points

- Priced at $1, it truly aligns with the concept: smart investing starts with smart spending.

- The integration of AI (like ChatGPT and DeepSeek) as co-editors and advisors is forward-looking and distinguishes this from traditional investing books.

- Many sections feel like a hybrid of personal coaching and DIY investing — a rare tone in finance books.

▓ Final Thoughts

This book is well-aligned for its purpose and price:

- **Approachable, practical**, and **authentic.**

- A **useful primer** that competes well with free articles or $20+ beginner guides.

Final Thoughts from DeepSeek:

Tony Pow's book delivers on its promise: a **budget-friendly, no-nonsense guide** for investing newcomers. Its strengths lie in simplicity and actionable steps, though it lacks depth for seasoned readers. The AI-assisted content is a novelty, but the real value is in the foundational advice—perfect for someone investing their "first dollar."

Rating: ★★★★☆ (4/5)

Recommendation: Highly

Reviewd on 5/28/2025

Review of "Momentum Investing 3rd Edition "

Strengths:
1. **Extensive Data & Performance Tracking** – You provide a thorough history of your momentum stock trades, including real-world examples and performance analysis, which adds credibility.
2. **Diverse Momentum Strategies** – You break momentum investing into multiple strategies, catering to different holding periods and risk tolerances.
3. **Sector Rotation & Market Timing** – The book successfully integrates sector rotation and market timing to enhance momentum strategies.
4. **Practical Implementation** – Step-by-step guides on using platforms like Finviz, Seeking Alpha, and Fidelity make it easy for readers to apply the strategies.
5. **Personal Investment Experience** – Your personal trading history and transparent performance records provide valuable lessons for readers.

Final Verdict:
This is an in-depth and practical guide for momentum investors, backed by real-world experience.

Review of "Using profitable investment sites" rated 8

Strengths

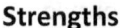 **Comprehensive Coverage** – The book provides in-depth discussions on various investment platforms, strategies, and techniques, covering fundamental and technical analysis, sector rotation, market timing, and more.

Practical Insights – You include personal investment experiences and strategies, making the content relatable and actionable for readers.

Structured for Different Investors – It caters to beginner, intermediate, and advanced investors, helping readers navigate content at their level.

Focus on Market Timing & Sector Rotation – These strategies can be useful for those looking to enhance returns beyond standard buy-and-hold approaches.

Use of Free and Paid Investment Tools – The book effectively highlights how to leverage platforms like Barron's, Finviz, and Seeking Alpha for research.

Final Verdict

Rating: 4/5

Your book is a **valuable resource for self-directed investors**, particularly those interested in using online tools for research and market timing. With tighter editing and better visual organization, it could become an even more **impactful investment guide.**

Review of "Investing successes and blunders"

Strengths:
1. **Practical Experience:** Your personal investing experiences, both successes and mistakes, add authenticity and credibility. Readers can learn from real-life examples rather than just theoretical concepts.
2. **Data-Driven Approach:** Your detailed performance tracking of stock picks and strategies over multiple years demonstrates a commitment to rigorous analysis.
3. **Market Timing Insights:** The emphasis on simple market timing techniques and avoiding common pitfalls, such as emotional investing and overreliance on government policies, is valuable.
4. **Sector-Specific Insights:** Your discussion of various market sectors, including AI, real estate, bonds, and commodities, helps readers understand different investment opportunities.

Risk Management: Your explanations of calculated vs. blind risks, the importance of diversification, and strategies like stop-loss orders are useful for investors at all levels.

Appendix 3 - Our window to the investing world

The paperback version of this chapter can be found in the following link.
http://ebmyth.blogspot.com/2013/11/web-sites.html

- **General**
  Wikipedia / Investopedia /Yahoo!Finance / MarketWatch / Cnnfn / Morningstar /CNBC / Bloomberg / WSJ / Barron's / Motley Fool / TheStreet
- **Evaluate stocks**
  Finviz / SeekingAlpha / MSN Money / Zacks / Daily Finance / ADR / Fidelity / Earnings Impact / OpenInsider / NYSE / NASDAQ / SEC / SEC for 10K and 10Q (quarterly) reports required to file for listed stocks in major exchanges.
- **Charts**
  BigCharts / FreeStockCharts / StockCharts /
- **Screens**
  Yahoo!Finance / Finviz / CNBC / Morningstar /
- **Besides stocks**
  123Jump / Hoover's Online / FINRA Bond Market Data / REIT / Commodity Futures / Option Industry
- **Vendors**
  AAII / Zacks / IBD / GuruFocus / VectorVest / Fidelity / Interactive Brokers / Merrill Lynch /
- **Economy.**
  Econday / EcoconStats / Federal Reserve / Economist /
- **Misc.**
  Dow Jones Indices / Russell / Wilshire / IRS / Wikinvest / ETF Database / ETF Trends / Nolo (estate planning) / AARP /

Appendix 4 - ETFs / Mutual Funds

What is an ETF
ETFs have basic differences from mutual funds: 1. Lower management expenses, 2. Trade ETFs same as stocks, and 3. Usually more diversified but not more selective than the related mutual funds such as NOBL vs FRDPX.

The major classifications of ETFs are 1. Simulating an index such as SPY, QQQ and DIA, 2. Simulating a sector such as XLE and SOXX, 3. Simulating an asset class such as GLD and SLV, 4. Simulating a country or a group of countries such as EWC and FXI, 5. Managed by a manager(s) such as ARKK, 6. Betting a market or sector to go down such as SH and PSQ, and 7. Leveraged (not recommended for beginners).

Fidelity: Index ETFs (https://www.fidelity.com/etfs/overview).
Wikipedia on ETF (http://en.wikipedia.org/wiki/Exchange-traded_fund).

List of ETFs
ETF database (Recommended): http://etfdb.com/
ETF Bloomberg: http://www.bloomberg.com/markets/etfs/
ETF Trends: http://www.etftrends.com/
A list of ETFs. Seeking Alpha.
http://etf.stock-encyclopedia.com/category/)
A list of contra ETFs (or bear ETFs)
http://www.tradermike.net/inverse-short-etfs-bearish-etf-funds/
Misc.: ETFGuide, ETFReplay
Fidelity low-cost index funds:
https://www.youtube.com/watch?v=zpKi4_IJvlY
Fidelity Annuity funds with performance data.
http://fundresearch.fidelity.com/annuities/category-performance-annual-total-returns-quarterly/FPRAI?refann=005
ETFs vs mutual funds;
https://www.youtube.com/watch?v=Vmz0CzlQvHk
Three ETFs: https://www.youtube.com/watch?v=MVi2RhpffuU

Other resources
Most subscription services offer research on ETFs. IBD has a strategy dedicated to ETFs and so does AAII to name a couple. Seeking Alpha has extensive resources for ETF including an ETF screener and investing ideas. So is ETFdb.

Not all ETFs are created equal
Check their performances and their expenses.

When to use or not to use ETFs
I prefer sector mutual funds in some industries, as they have many bad stocks such as drug industry, banks, miners and insurers. Most mutual funds cannot time the market.

When you believe a sector is heading up (or contra ETF for heading down), but you do not have time to do research on specific stocks, buy an ETF for the sector; it is same for the market.

Half ETF

Taking out half of the stocks that score below the average in an index ETF could beat the same full ETF itself. I call it HETF (half the ETF). You heard it here first. After a decade, at least one company has a similar product.

To illustrate, sort the expected P/E (not including stocks with negative earnings) in ascending order and only include the stocks on the first half. Add more fundamental metrics. It will take a few minutes.

Disadvantages of ETFs
- When you have two stocks in a sector ETF one good one and one bad one, the ETF treats them the same. Stock pickers would buy the one that has a better appreciation potential.
- Sometimes the return could be misleading due to stock rotation. To illustrate this, on August 29, 2012, SHLD was replaced by LYB in a sector fund. SHLD was down by 4% and LYB was up by 4% primarily due to the switch. Unless you sell and buy at the right time (which is impossible), your return would not match the ETF's returns due to the replacement.
- Ensure the performance matches the corresponding index; it is hard due to excluding dividends.

Advantages of ETFs
- We have demonstrated that you can beat the market by using market timing. Between 2000 and Nov., 2013, you only exit and reenter the market 3 times and the result is astonishing.
- It is easy to rotate a sector vs. buying/selling all of the stocks in this sector. Rotating a sector is the same as trading a stock.
- The risk is spread out, and your portfolio is diversified especially for a market ETF or buying three or more ETFs in different sectors.
- Periodically the bad stocks in most funds are replaced by better stocks.
- Eliminate the time in researching stocks.

Leveraged ETFs

I do not recommend them. Some are 2x, 3x and even higher. They're too risky for beginners. However, when you are very sure or your tested strategy has very low drawdown, you may want to use them to improve performance. Most leveraged ETFs and contra ETFs have higher fees.

My basic ETF tables
I include some contra ETFs, mutual funds and Fidelity's annuity. Some of these may be interesting to you. Most Vanguard's ETFs have lower fees.

ETFs and funds come and go. Some ideas and classifications are my own interpretation. Refer to ETFdb for updated information. Not responsible for any error. Check out the ETF or fund before you take any action.

I prefer VFINX over SPY for the lower fees; both simulate the S&P 500 index. The stocks in the ETF can be either equally weighted or weighted by market caps. The latter is more like using momentum strategy, as the rising stocks usually have larger market caps. The index usually kicks out some poor-performing stocks and replaced them with better stocks. These ETFs are suited for long-term investing without constant reviews.

Table by market cap:

Category	ETF	Mutual Funds	Fidelity's Annuity	Contra ETF	Alternate
Size:					
Large Cap	DIA			DOG	
	SPY			SH	VOO VFINX RSP FXAIX
	QQQ			PSQ	FNCMX
	RYH				
Blend	IWD	BEQGX			
Growth	SPYG	FBGRX			FSPGX
Value	SPYV	DOGGX			FLCOX
Dividend	NOBL	FRDPX			
	VYM				
Mid Cap			FNBSC	MYY	
Blend	MDY	VSEQX			
Growth		STDIX			
		BPTRX			
Value		FSMVX			
Small Cap			FPRGC	SBB	FSSNX

Blend	IWM	HDPSX			
Growth		PRDSX			FECGX
Value		SKSEX			FISVX
Micro	IWC				
Multi					
Blend		VDEOX			
Growth		VHCOX			
Value		TCLCX			
Total					FSKAX VTI
Bond					
Long Term (20)	VLV	BTTTX		TBF	
Mid Term (7 – 10)	VCIT	FSTGX			
Short Term (1 – 3 yrs.)	VCSH	THOPX			
Total	BOND	PONDX			
Corp Invest Grade	VCIT	NTHEX			
High Yield (junk)	PHB	SPHIX			
Muni	MUB	Check state			
Special situation					
Buy back	PKW				

Table by sectors:

Sector	ETF	Mutual Funds	Fidelity's Annuity
Banking[1]		FSRBK	
Regional	IAT		
Biotech	IBB	FBIOX	
	XBI	Large	
Consumer Dis.	XLY	FSCPX	FVHAC
Consumer Staple	XLP	FDFAX	FCSAC
Defense + Aero	PPA		
Finance	KIE	FIDSX	FONNC
	IYF		
Energy	XLE	FSENX	FJLLC
Energy Service		FSESX	
Farm	DBA		
Gold	GLD	FSAGX	BAR
Gold Miner	GDX	VGPMX	
Health Care	IYH	FSPHX	FPDRC

	VHT	VGHCX	
House Builder	ITB	FSHOX	
Industrial	IYJ	FCYIX	FBALC
Material	VAW	FSDPX	GSG
	IYM		
Natural Gas	UNG		
Oil	USO		
Oil Service	OIH	FSESX	
Oil Exploration	XOP		
Real Estate	VNQ	FRIFX	FFWLC
REIT	VNQ		
Retail	RTH	FSRPX	
	XRT		
Regional bank	KRE	FSRBX	
Semi Conduct	SMH		
Software	XSW	FSCSX	
	IGV		
Technology	XLK	FSPTX	FYENC
	FDN	FBSOX	
		ROGSX	
Telecomm.	VOX	FSTCX	FVTAC
Transport	XTN		
	IYT		
Utilities	XLU	FSUTX	FKMSC
Wireless		FWRLX	

Footnote. [1] Also check Finance.

Table by countries outside the USA:

Country	ETF	Mutual Funds	Fidelity's Annuity	Alternate
Australia	EWA			
Brazil	EWZ			
Canada	EWC	FICDX		
China	FXI	FHKCX		
EAFE	EFA			
Emerging	VWO	FEMEX	FEMAC	FPADX
Europe	VGK	FIEUX		
Global	KXI	PGVFX		
Greece	GREK			
India	INDY	MINDX		
Indonesia	EIDO			
Latin America	ILF	FLATX		
Nordic		FNORX		
Hong Kong	EWH			

Japan	EWJ	FJPNX		
S. Africa	EZA			
S. Korea	EWY	MAKOX		
Singapore	EWS			
Taiwan	EWT			
Turkey	TUR			
United Kingdom	EWU			
Foreign:				
Combination				
Intern. Div.	IDV			FTIHX
Small Cap	SCZ			
Value	EFV			
Europe	VGK			

Appendix 5 - Links

The following may be repeated from the articles and it is for your convenience. To illustrate, Under YouTube (or Investopedia), search "Finviz". Some links have permanent values such as most articles from Wikipedia and Investopedia. Others reflect current events such as the current market. Learn from them and act when the current events have similar descriptions. For the printed versions and updated links, enter the following in your browser: https://tonyp4idea.blogspot.com/2023/02/links-in-my-books.html

Beginners

Common mistakes: https://www.youtube.com/watch?v=zkNueyFs8zQ

Best Vanguard ETFs https://www.youtube.com/watch?v=mSEyghlZchQ

Buy stocks/ETFs: https://www.youtube.com/watch?v=4vjkeC_4EmU

Screener

Finviz https://www.youtube.com/watch?v=cHNUMPgEYGY

Recommended YouTube: https://www.youtube.com/watch?v=CJoN7wLfWNo
PEG: http://en.wikipedia.org/wiki/PEG_ratio
Short %:
http://www.investopedia.com/university/shortselling/shortselling1.asp#axzz2LNDvpemo
Openinsider: http://www.openinsider.com/
Finviz: http://Finviz.com/
terms: http://www.Finviz.com/help/screener.ashx
Insider Cow: http://www.insidercow.com/
Current Ratio: http://en.wikipedia.org/wiki/Current_ratio
Cash Flow: https://www.youtube.com/watch?v=1v8hRZ36--c
Balance sheet: https://www.youtube.com/watch?v=DZjU0CHKyV4
How to find quality stocks.
http://seekingalpha.com/article/2381395-how-to-identify-quality-stocks-and-is-there-really-alpha-to-be-had

Investing strategies

Inflation: https://www.youtube.com/watch?v=Zpthvpy3UKg\

Swing: https://www.youtube.com/watch?v=C9EQkA7uVU8
https://www.youtube.com/watch?v=a_wpfSXRSjo
https://www.youtube.com/watch?v=M8sNMhPJIN

Momentum: https://www.youtube.com/watch?v=PpUlOyZrl9
Penny stocks: https://www.youtube.com/watch?v=u7xZ3kF62u4

Scanning https://www.youtube.com/watch?v=7iZpWmwBheI

Peter lynch 2023: https://www.youtube.com/watch?v=CK1AkVVVXu8

Charlie: https://www.youtube.com/watch?v=8g2B6QJ2FEc
Dividend ETFs: https://www.youtube.com/watch?v=64NEiyoNBIM

- Innovative   sectors:
  https://www.youtube.com/watch?v=LI1hMX8qtHg

Trading stocks
Beginners: https://www.youtube.com/watch?v=aod3cyUEu4k
Covered call https://www.youtube.com/watch?v=dzMOnI4Eh04

Tax Avoidance: http://en.wikipedia.org/wiki/Tax_avoidance
Tax Law: http://en.wikipedia.org/wiki/Income_tax_%28U.S.%29
Without paying (gift tax):
http://en.wikipedia.org/wiki/Gift_tax_in_the_United_States#Gift_tax_exemptions
http://www.irs.gov/Businesses/Small-Businesses-&-Self-Employed/What%27s-New---Estate-and-Gift-Tax
AMT: http://en.wikipedia.org/wiki/Alternative_minimum_tax
Estate planning fun. http://tonyp4idea.blogspot.com/2014/08/estate-planning-101-for-me.html
Taxes on stocks: https://www.youtube.com/watch?v=EKYMbsjUUtE
Tax avoidance: https://www.youtube.com/watch?v=tXou5pM7zh0
Capital gain: https://www.youtube.com/watch?v=ezPs4ibFsNU&t=2678s
Trading course: https://www.youtube.com/watch?v=8sbfrusR5Eo
How safe our brokers. https://www.youtube.com/watch?v=wz64z1YuL0A

Fidelity funds: https://www.youtube.com/watch?v=xdEunmLrhb4
Fidelity core money market fund:
https://www.youtube.com/watch?v=KU6HYRHj3jg

Government bond default? https://www.youtube.com/watch?v=wMxj6iB92ZA
Broker CDs (Recommended): https://www.youtube.com/watch?v=zhEiyW2N7KE
Money market fund: https://www.youtube.com/watch?v=N53wZ_80abU

Economy
YouTube video (highly recommended):
https://www.youtube.com/watch?v=Q6NIDJZdQH4

What will the world be in 5 years (2027).
https://www.youtube.com/watch?v=LzipwDQBUyc

Inflation and interest rate:
https://www.youtube.com/watch?v=q8KJSNyAHLE

Wealth gap widens with low interest rate:
https://www.youtube.com/watch?v=t6m49vNjEGs
Investing helps the economy:
https://www.youtube.com/watch?v=W6ICRTqsxk8

#Filler: Honey, my book can play music.
https://www.youtube.com/watch?v=HxGT5z6d-GA&list=PLMZa6mP7jZ2b1otqG4tfbgZpLEdh6YiNF